Citing Audiovisual Sources 97

  7a A Film *97*
  7b A Slide Set or Filmstrip *98*
  7c A Television Broadcast *98*
  7d A Radio Broadcast *99*
  7e A Recording *99*
  7f An Interview *100*
  7g A Lecture or Speech *101*
  7h A Work of Art *101*
  7i A Map, Graph, Table, or Chart *101*

Citing Electronic Sources 103

  8a An Article in an Online Journal *106*
  8b An Article in an Online Magazine *106*
  8c An Article in an Online Newspaper *106*
  8d An Article in an Online Newsletter *107*
  8e An Online Book *107*
  8f An Online Dissertation or Thesis *108*
  8g An Online Abstract *108*
  8h An Article in an Online Encyclopedia or Other Reference Work *109*
  8i A Website or Scholarly Project *109*
  8j An Online Transcript of a Lecture or Speech *110*
  8k An Online Map, Graph, Table, or Chart *110*
  8l A CD-ROM Source *111*
  8m An Email Interview *111*
  8n An Online Video *112*
  8o An Audio Podcast *112*
  8p A Posting—Blog, Discussion Group, Facebook, or Twitter *113*

POCKET GUIDE TO APA STYLE

SEVENTH EDITION

Robert Perrin

INDIANA STATE UNIVERSITY

Australia • Brazil • Mexico • Singapore •
United Kingdom • United States

Pocket Guide to APA Style, Seventh Edition
Robert Perrin

Product Team Manager:
 Catherine Van Der Laan

Product Manager:
 Nancy Tran

Product Assistant:
 Madeline Blackburn

Executive Marketing Manager:
 Kina Lara

Senior Content Manager:
 Rachel Kerns

Learning Designer:
 Leslie Taggart

In-House SME:
 Anne Alexander

Digital Delivery Lead:
 Matt Altieri

IP Analyst:
 Ashley Maynard

IP Project Manager:
 Nick Barrows

Production Service:
 SPi Global

Art Director:
 Lizz Anderson

Cover Designer: Lizz Anderson

Cover Image: Chief Crow Daria/Shutterstock.com

© 2021, 2018, 2015 Cengage Learning, Inc.

ALL RIGHTS RESERVED. No part of this work covered by the copyright herein may be reproduced or distributed in any form or by any means, except as permitted by U.S. copyright law, without the prior written permission of the copyright owner.

For product information and technology assistance, contact us at **Cengage Customer & Sales Support, 1-800-354-9706 or support.cengage.com.**

For permission to use material from this text or product, submit all requests online at **www.cengage.com/permissions.**

Library of Congress Control Number: 2020909287

Student Edition:
ISBN: 978-0-357-63296-3

Cengage Learning
200 Pier 4 Boulevard
Boston, MA 02210
USA

Cengage is a leading provider of customized learning solutions with employees residing in nearly 40 different countries and sales in more than 125 countries around the world. Find your local representative at **www.cengage.com.**

Cengage Learning products are represented in Canada by Nelson Education, Ltd.

To learn more about Cengage platforms and services, register or access your online learning solution, or purchase materials for your course, visit **www.cengage.com.**

Printed in Mexico
Print Number: 02 Print Year: 2020

Contents

Preface ix

1 Writing Scholarly Papers 1
- 1a Subject and Topic 1
- 1b Thesis Statements, Hypotheses, or Stated Objectives 3
- 1c Research Goals 3
- 1d Research Methods 5
- 1e Evaluating Sources 10
- 1f Note-Taking 14
- 1g Plagiarism 17
- 1h Planning 21
- 1i Writing Strategies 22

2 Preparing APA Manuscripts 27
- 2a Parts of the Manuscript 27
- 2b Footnotes 32
- 2c General Manuscript Guidelines 36

3 Following APA Editorial Style 41
- 3a Punctuation and Mechanics 41
- 3b General Style 54
- 3c Word Choice 58

4 Preparing the Reference List and Parenthetical Citations 63
- 4a The Reference List—An Overview 63
- 4b Information for APA Entries 64
- 4c Format for APA Entries 66
- 4d Alphabetizing the Reference List 69
- 4e Parenthetical Citations 71
- 4f Quotations 74

5 Citing Periodicals 79
- 5a An Article in a Journal 80
- 5b An Abstract 80
- 5c An Article in a Monthly Magazine 81

- 5d An Article in a Weekly Magazine 81
- 5e An Article in a Newspaper 81
- 5f An Article in a Newsletter 82
- 5g An Editorial 82
- 5h A Letter to the Editor 83
- 5i A Review 83
- 5j A Secondary Source 84

6 Citing Books and Other Separately Published Materials 85

- 6a A Book by One Author 86
- 6b A Book by Two or More Authors 86
- 6c A Book With No Author Named 87
- 6d A Book With an Organization as Author 87
- 6e An Edition Other Than the First 88
- 6f An Edited Collection 88
- 6g An Original Selection in an Edited Collection 88
- 6h A Previously Published Selection in an Edited Collection 89
- 6i A Revised or Enlarged Edition 90
- 6j A Reprinted Book 90
- 6k A Multivolume Work 90
- 6l An Article in an Encyclopedia or Other Reference Work 91
- 6m A Translation 92
- 6n A Government Document—Committee, Commission, Department 92
- 6o A Preface, Introduction, Foreword, Epilogue, or Afterword 93
- 6p A Monograph 93
- 6q A Pamphlet, Brochure, or Fact Sheet 94
- 6r An Unpublished Dissertation 94
- 6s Published Proceedings From a Conference 94
- 6t Multiple Works by the Same Author 95
- 6u A Secondary Source 96

7 Citing Audiovisual Sources 97

- 7a A Film 97
- 7b A Slide Set or Filmstrip 98

7c A Television Broadcast 98
7d A Radio Broadcast 99
7e A Recording 99
7f An Interview 100
7g A Lecture or Speech 101
7h A Work of Art 101
7i A Map, Graph, Table, or Chart 101

8 Citing Electronic Sources 103

8a An Article in an Online Journal 106
8b An Article in an Online Magazine 106
8c An Article in an Online Newspaper 106
8d An Article in an Online Newsletter 107
8e An Online Book 107
8f An Online Dissertation or Thesis 108
8g An Online Abstract 108
8h An Article in an Online Encyclopedia or Other Reference Work 109
8i A Website or Scholarly Project 109
8j An Online Transcript of a Lecture or Speech 110
8k An Online Map, Graph, Table, or Chart 110
8l A CD-ROM Source 111
8m An Email Interview 111
8n An Online Video 112
8o An Audio Podcast 112
8p A Posting—Blog, Discussion Group, Facebook, or Twitter 113

9 Examining Sample Papers 115

"Beyond Birth Order: Recognizing Other Variables" 115
"Students' Reactions to Kinds of Test Questions: A Piece of the Test-Anxiety Puzzle" 127

Appendix A Preparing an Annotated Bibliography 139

- A1 Following Format Guidelines 139
- A2 Thinking About the Content of Annotations 140
- A3 Planning Annotations 141
- A4 Creating the Elements of an Annotated Bibliography 141

Appendix B Preparing PowerPoint and Poster Presentations 147

- B1 Preparing a PowerPoint Presentation 147
- B2 Preparing a Poster Presentation 155

Appendix C Addressing Technical Issues in Writing 159

- C1 Fragments 159
- C2 Comma Splices and Fused Sentences 161
- C3 Pronoun Reference 162
- C4 Pronoun Case 164
- C5 Positioning Modifiers 169
- C6 Active and Passive Voice 171
- C7 Possessives and Contractions 172
- C8 Outlining 174

Index 179

Preface

Pocket Guide to APA Style, 7th edition, is designed for students who need to write, document, and present papers in American Psychological Association style. This convenient and easy-to-use guide draws on the principles described in the seventh edition of the *Publication Manual of the American Psychological Association* (2020). What sets *Pocket Guide to APA Style* apart from the lengthy *Publication Manual* is its overriding goal: This text presents the principles in a brief yet complete and easy-to-use manner. The guide is ideal for undergraduates who are working with APA style for the first time. Yet graduate students and working professionals will also appreciate its user-friendliness. To enhance its use, *Pocket Guide to APA Style* incorporates these helpful features.

- **Writing Scholarly Papers: An Overview** The introductory chapter of *Pocket Guide* describes basic researching and writing methods, serving as a brief review.

- **Manuscript Preparation** In one coherent chapter, *Pocket Guide* describes and illustrates all elements of an APA manuscript.

- **Editorial Style** In one convenient chapter, *Pocket Guide* explains APA guidelines for punctuation and mechanics (periods, quotation marks, capitalization, number style, and so on), general writing style (transitions, verb tense, and so on), and word choice (jargon, biased language, and so on).

- **Separate Documentation Chapters** For easy use, *Pocket Guide* provides separate chapters to explain reference-list entries for periodicals, books and other separately published materials, audiovisual sources, and electronic sources.

- **Reference-List Entries and Parenthetical Citations** Chapters 4 through 8 include guidelines for documenting 56 kinds of sources, with 114 sample reference-list entries. These samples are followed by corresponding in-text citations.

- **Sample Papers** Two complete sample papers are included in *Pocket Guide*, one argumentative and one experimental; both include annotations related to manuscript form and issues of writing. Several sample pages also show APA's new guidelines for formatting student papers.

- **A Discussion of Plagiarism** With its student focus, *Pocket Guide* includes a discussion of plagiarism and ways to avoid it.

- **Preparing an Annotated Bibliography** A new appendix discusses the format for an annotated bibliography, as well as ideas for developing and organizing the content of the annotations. A sample is included.

- **Appendices** Included in *Pocket Guide* are three appendices: one provides instructions for preparing an annotated bibliography, one describes effective ways to prepare PowerPoint and poster presentations, and one covers the essential technical issues writers encounter across the disciplines.

MindTap for *Pocket Guide to APA Style*

MindTap for *Pocket Guide to APA Style* is the digital learning solution that gives you complete control of your course—to provide engaging content, challenge every individual, and build students' confidence. It gives you complete ownership of your content and your students' learning experience. You can add your own comments to the e-book and your own materials to the learning path, and you can move, rename, and delete content to ensure that your course is exactly how you want it. Visual analytics track your students' progress and engagement.

This MindTap includes the following features:

- **Aplia homework** for every chapter provides auto-graded exercises that give students immediate, detailed feedback for their answers.
- **Auto-graded Activities** cover a wide range of composition topics, from writing an essay to critical thinking to how to correct fragments. Students get three tries on each activity, giving them every chance to successfully complete the activity.
- **Focused Support for Key Topics** provides a complete learning path for each of 9 of the most difficult topics for students to understand in the areas of argument, evaluating sources, and critical thinking. Each learning path includes textual instruction, video examples of students applying the concepts, auto-graded review activities, a student essay, and two professional essays with discussion questions.
- **Just in Time Plus** provides students with foundational help on reading, writing, grammar, and research topics. Each unit includes a short instructional video, several pages of textual instruction, and an auto-graded assignment to ensure that students grasped the material.
- **Resources for Teaching** provides support materials to help you plan and teach your course, including a video on how to customize your MindTap course.

Acknowledgments

My work on the seventh edition of *Pocket Guide* was pleasant and productive because of the supportive, knowledgeable assistance of Senior Content Manager Rachel Kerns at Cengage. I also thank Praveen Kumar RS, Senior Project Manager at SPi Global, for his careful handling of the production work.

As always, I wish to thank Judy, Jenny, Chris, and Kate for their encouragement.

R. P.

1 Writing Scholarly Papers

Chapter Objectives:

- Learn about (or reconsider) strategies for selecting a topic and formulating a thesis statement, hypothesis, or stated objective.
- Learn about (or review) basic approaches to research.
- Consider ways to evaluate research sources of all kinds.
- Learn (or reconsider) techniques for taking notes from sources.
- Analyze the causes and repercussions of plagiarism and learn the means to avoid it.
- Learn (or review) strategies for planning, drafting, and revising your paper.

The research process is a complex combination of thinking, searching, reading, evaluating, writing, and revising. It is, in many ways, a highly personal process because writers approach research activities by drawing on different skills and past experiences. Yet researchers often follow a series of connected phases (which nonetheless occur in a different order for different people).

This chapter reviews, in a brief way, the common steps that most researchers go through. If you are an experienced researcher, you can use this chapter as a "refresher." If your research experiences are limited, consider each discussion carefully as you proceed with your work.

1a Subject and Topic

Research begins with a subject. In some academic contexts, you may choose the subject yourself, usually with the instructor's approval. But in other contexts, you may be required to choose a topic from a small number of suggested topics or be assigned a topic with a predetermined focus.

Guidelines for Assessing General Subjects

As you select potential subjects for your research (broad categories such as test anxiety, internet crime, the effects of divorce, and so on), keep in mind these practical and important principles.

- **Interest.** When possible, select a subject that interests you. Do not spend time researching a subject that does not make you curious.
- **Length.** Select a subject that can be adequately treated within the length requirements of the assignment. You may have to expand or reduce the scope of your subject to match these length constraints.
- **Materials.** Select a subject for which you can find materials of the kind identified in the assignment. Be aware that you can use libraries other than your own for your research and that the internet provides access to a broad range of materials, both traditional and nontraditional.
- **Challenge.** Select a subject that challenges you but that does not require technical or other specialized knowledge you may not have time to acquire.
- **Uniqueness.** Select a subject that is not overused. Overly familiar subjects stimulate little interest, and materials are soon depleted.
- **Perspective.** Select a subject you can approach in a fresh, interesting way. Readers will appreciate your efforts to examine subjects from new perspectives.

Narrow Topic

In most instances, you will need to narrow your large subject (test anxiety, for example) to a specific topic (test anxiety among middle school students) so that you can research selectively and address the issue in a focused way.

To discover ways to narrow a broad subject to a specific topic, skim general reference materials, paying particular attention to recurrent themes, details, and ideas. Then consider establishing a focus using selected strategies for limiting topics.

- **Time.** Restrict the subject to a specific, manageable time span—for example, school violence in the 2000s.
- **Place.** Restrict the subject to a specific location—for example, health care in rural areas of the United States.
- **Special circumstance.** Restrict the subject to a specific context or circumstance—for example, achievement testing for college admissions.
- **Specific population.** Restrict the subject to address its effects on a selected group of people—for example, depression among older adults.

1b Thesis Statements, Hypotheses, or Stated Objectives

To clarify the central goal of your writing, present your ideas in one of three alternative ways.

Thesis Statement

A thesis statement, sometimes called a problem statement, is a declarative statement (usually one but sometimes two or more sentences) that clarifies your specific topic, presents your opinion of (not merely facts about) the topic, and incorporates qualifications or limitations necessary to understand your views.

> Although the effects of birth order are always evident to some degree, other variables also affect personality, intelligence, and socialization.

Hypothesis

A hypothesis is a conjectural statement that guides an argument or investigation; it can be explored (and potentially proved or disproved) by examining data related to your topic. Conditional in nature, a hypothesis is assessed using available information.

> Students who delay work on major research projects until the last week are more likely to plagiarize than are students who begin their work early.

Stated Objective

A stated objective is a brief, well-focused statement that describes a research paper that presents information. Unsubtle and not arguable, it must define the topic clearly and narrow the topic when necessary.

> I will share a brief history of airport security in the United States, from the 1940s to the present day.

1c Research Goals

Although most research is prompted by specific academic or job-related requirements, you should also think broadly about the goals for your work, recognizing that research provides multifaceted learning experiences.

Course-Related Goals

Course-related goals are broad in scope and establish the foundation of your research work.

- **Using the library.** Library research should take advantage of a full range of sources, as well as the electronic means to locate them (see pages 5–9).
- **Using the internet for academic purposes.** Research requires that you learn to use the internet selectively for scholarly purposes, which involves learning to evaluate the credibility and value of online materials (see pages 9–10).
- **Assessing source materials.** In a global way, research depends on evaluating materials critically to ensure that you use sources that credibly support your ideas (see pages 10–14).
- **Taking notes.** Research requires you to record ideas and information from your sources carefully and completely so that you can use them appropriately in your writing (see pages 14–17).
- **Responding effectively to opposing views.** Fair-minded research acknowledges and uses opposing views to maintain a balanced perspective.
- **Synthesizing ideas.** Effective research blends information and ideas from a variety of sources, thereby creating a comprehensive presentation that is better or fairer or clearer than the presentation in individual sources.
- **Incorporating material into writing.** Effective research leads to writing that incorporates ideas and information with clarity, accuracy, and style (see pages 22–25 and Section 4f).
- **Citing sources accurately.** Research requires you to give proper credit to the people whose ideas and information you have used; this technically focused process requires attention to detail (see Chapters 4–8).

Professional Goals

Professional goals develop from the process of establishing a working knowledge in your field of study. As such, they focus on the acquisition of knowledge and specific skills.

- **Learning to use specific sources.** Research in each discipline requires familiarity with the kinds of sources that are respected and commonly used.
- **Demonstrating discipline-specific knowledge.** Research in each discipline builds upon accepted information that you must be able to incorporate fluently.

- **Using specialized formats.** Each discipline's research incorporates unique formats that you must learn to follow.
- **Using specialized writing styles.** Research in each discipline depends on specific stylistic patterns for presenting ideas and information.

Personal Goals

Personal goals concentrate on degrees of knowledge, improvement, sophistication, and experience. Although they are less easily quantified than goals matched to courses, they are also important.

- **Learning about a subject.** Exploring a subject through research improves your knowledge of your discipline.
- **Improving skills.** Conducting research gives you the opportunity not only to use your early research work but also to develop more sophisticated skills.
- **Expanding experiences.** Research work allows for varied kinds of personal growth.

1d Research Methods

Methods of research vary depending on the project, but most projects require multidimensional work with a variety of sources. To complete such projects, take advantage of a full range of strategies.

The Library

Learn to use all features of your library, especially familiarizing yourself with the research areas that you will most commonly use.

- **Reference.** General source materials—dictionaries, fact books, encyclopedias, indexes, guides, bibliographies, and so on—that can guide your preliminary research. (Most reference materials are now available in electronic form.)
- **Catalog (computer).** Computer clusters where you can secure the records of library materials. (Almost all computer catalogs can be accessed from other locations.)
- **Stacks.** Bookcases where print materials (bound periodicals, books, and so on) are stored according to a classification system.
- **Current periodicals.** Recent copies of journals, magazines, and newspapers. (Most periodicals are now available in electronic form.)

- **Government documents.** Printed materials from national, state, and local government departments and agencies—books, monographs, reports, pamphlets, and so on. (Most government documents are available in electronic form through government websites.)
- **Microforms.** Microfilm and microfiche materials. (Many of these materials have been converted to digital forms.)
- **Media.** Audiovisual sources—DVDs, Blu-rays, CDs, and so on.
- **New books.** The area where new books are displayed before being placed in the general collection.
- **Special collections.** The area where rare books, archival materials, and other special sources are located.
- **Special libraries.** Discipline-specific collections that are housed in sublibraries.

Periodical Databases and Online Catalogs

Periodical databases (online indexes) allow you to gather technical information about—and frequently view full texts of—articles in journals, magazines, and newspapers. Online catalogs (electronic search systems) allow you to gather technical information about books, monographs, government documents, and other materials in the library's collection. Both periodical databases and online catalogs provide access to descriptive material about sources through keyword search techniques.

Keyword searching uses easily recognizable words and phrases (often in combination) to access sources. Computer systems search for keywords in titles, tables of contents, and other descriptive materials and then display "matches." To locate a broad range of materials, use alternative phrases (*collaborative learning, collaboration, team research*, and so on) as you conduct searches. Also explore Library of Congress listings, available online at most libraries, to discover unique category descriptions. For example, the Library of Congress system does not use the fairly conventional expression *medical ethics*; rather, its category notation is *medical care—moral and ethical aspects*.

Information About Periodicals

Most libraries subscribe to a variety of periodical databases. These databases vary in design and format, but all provide a wide range of information about articles in journals, magazines, and newspapers. Most databases provide information about the following elements.

- **Article title.** Full title and subtitle of the article (listed first because some articles have no attributed authors).
- **Author.** Full name of the author (or authors).
- **Affiliation.** Professional affiliation (university, institution, and so on) of the author (or authors).
- **Periodical title.** Title of the journal, magazine, or newspaper.
- **Volume and issue number.** Volume (which indicates the number of years that a periodical has been published) and issue number (which refers to the specific issue in which the article appeared) for journals and magazines, but not for newspapers.
- **Number of pages.** Total number of pages of the article (in the original print format); alternatively, the starting page of the article.
- **Date.** Month/year, month/day/year, or season/year of publication.
- **ISSN number.** The 8-digit International Standard Serial Number (ISSN) of the article.
- **Abstract.** A short but detailed overview of the article, emphasizing key ideas and briefly explaining procedures for publication.
- **Language.** The language in which the article is written (English, Japanese, Farsi, and so on).
- **Document type.** A brief description of the article (feature article, journal article, review, and so on).
- **Classification.** The article's subclassification within the discipline (child psychology, educational psychology, cognitive psychology, and so on).
- **Subjects or keywords.** Subjects or specific phrases in the article (medical ethics, juvenile delinquency, test anxiety, and so on).
- **Publisher or source.** A description of the periodical (periodical, peer-reviewed journal, and so on).
- **DOI.** The digital object identifier (DOI) assigned to the article.
- **Formats for articles.** Formats available for selected articles: HTML, PDF, summary, and abstract (see page 8).
- **Database.** The name of the database that provides the digital record.
- **Options.** Choices for using the database record for the source (Save, Print, Email, and so on).

In addition to these common elements, individual databases provide other detailed information: the author's email address, the database access number, the country of publication, the database identification number, the document URL, the number of references, the word count, the research techniques (tests and measures, age of research subjects, methodology), the publication history (date submitted, revised, and accepted), and the copyright.

You may never need all of the information provided in a database listing, but reviewing the full range of material will allow you to evaluate a source before retrieving it.

Format Options (Within a Periodical Database)

- **HTML.** Hypertext markup language. A digitized version of the article available on a website.
- **PDF.** Portable document format. A page-by-page scanned image of the source as it appeared in print, available as a single file.

Information About Books and Other Library-Based Materials

Online catalogs provide standardized information about each source in the library's collection.

- **Author.** Full name of the author (or authors).
- **Title.** Full title of the source, including subtitles.
- **Facts of publication.** City, publisher, and copyright date.
- **ISBN.** The 10- or 13-digit International Standard Book Number (ISBN) if the source is a book.
- **Technical description.** Specific features—edition, number of pages, use of illustrations, book size, and so on.
- **Format.** Description of the source (book, book with CD, book with audiotape, and so on).
- **Subject classification.** Library of Congress classification, both primary and secondary.
- **Notes.** Descriptions of special features (bibliography, index, appendices, and so on).
- **Location.** Location of the source in the library's collection (general collection, special collection, or specialty library).

- **Call number.** Classification number assigned to the source (indicating where the source is located in the collection).
- **Number of items.** Number of items (three volumes, one volume with CD-ROM, and so on).
- **Status.** Information on whether the source is checked out, on reserve, on loan, and so on.
- **Options.** Choices for using the online catalog record for the source (Save, Print, Email, Add to List, and so on).

Many online catalogs provide links to websites like *Google Books*, which provide other kinds of information: reviews from readers, sources for buying books (Amazon.com, Barnesandnoble.com), a list of other books that refer to the source, other available editions, the table of contents, the length, the cost, and so on.

The Internet

Internet research may lead you to a scholarly project (a university- or institution-based, scholarly site that provides a wide range of materials such as full-text books, research data, and visual materials), an information database (a site that offers statistical information from governmental agencies, research institutions, or nonprofit corporations), or a website (a site designed to share information or ideas, forward a political agenda, promote a product, or advocate a position). (See pages 12–13.)

To navigate an internet site successfully and to gather crucial information for a reference-list entry, learn about the key elements of an internet home page.

- **Electronic address (URL).** Uniform resource locator—the combination of elements that locates the source (for example, https://aagponline.org is the URL for the website of the American Association for Geriatric Psychiatry).
- **Official title.** Title and subtitle of the site.
- **Author, host, editor, or webmaster.** Person (or people) responsible for developing and maintaining the site, if identified.
- **Affiliation or sponsorship.** Person, group, organization, or agency that develops and maintains the material on the site.
- **Location.** Place (city, school, organization, institution, agency, and so on) from which the site originates.
- **Posting date or update.** Date on which the site was first posted or most recently updated (revised).

- **"About This Site."** Description of how the site was developed, a rationale for it, or information about those involved with the site.
- **Site directory.** Electronic table of contents for the site.

1e   Evaluating Sources

Because all sources are not equally useful, you should analyze them and select the ones best suited to your research. This ongoing process requires continued assessments and reassessments.

Print Sources (and Their Electronic Counterparts)

Print sources—journals, magazines, newspapers, books, and so on—have traditionally been the mainstay of most research; today, many of these sources are also available in electronic formats. Whether available in print or available in an alternative electronic format, these sources are the easiest to evaluate because of their familiarity.

- **Author's credentials.** Determine whether academic degrees, scholarly training, current research, affiliations, and other published work establish the author's authority.
- **Appropriate focus.** Determine whether the source addresses the topic in a way that matches your emphasis. Consider literature reviews to establish scholarly context and empirical studies to incorporate recent primary research.
- **Professionally affiliated periodicals.** Generally, use professional journals with strong organizational affiliations; furthermore, note that peer-reviewed journals (those that publish works only after they have been recommended by a panel of expert reviewers) offer more credibility than non-peer-reviewed journals (See page 11.)
- **Popular periodicals.** Although most research should come from scholarly journals, it is sometimes helpful to include information from popular or trade periodicals to show how information and ideas are presented to general, rather than professional, audiences. Choose topic-specific, rather than general-interest, magazines. Choose major newspapers for topics of international or national importance, but choose regional or local newspapers for issues of regional or local importance.
- **Sufficient coverage.** Determine whether the source sufficiently covers the topic by examining its table of contents, reviewing the index, and skimming a portion of the text.

Evaluating Sources

- **Reputable publishers.** University, academic, or trade presses publish most of the books you will use, which generally ensures their credibility. Note also that publishers often specialize in books related to particular subjects. For example, Jossey-Bass specializes in materials in higher education and adult learning, and Wiley-Blackwell publishes a substantial number of books related to medicine.
- **Publication date.** For many topics, sources more than 5 or 10 years old have limited value. However, consider establishing historical context by using older sources.
- **Useful supplementary materials.** Look for in-text illustrations, tables, charts, graphs, diagrams, bibliographies, case studies, or collections of additional readings.
- **Appropriate writing style.** Skim a potential source to see how it is developed (with facts, examples, description, or narration); also consider whether the author's style is varied, clear, informative, and persuasive.

SCHOLARLY JOURNALS	POPULAR MAGAZINES
Affiliated with a professional organization	Affiliated with a news or other organization
Reviewed by peers in the professional discipline	Reviewed by editorial staff
Intended for specialists in the field	Intended for nonspecialists
Intended to advance knowledge in a field	Intended to inform, entertain, or persuade
Academic publisher	Commercial publisher
SAMPLE	SAMPLE
Review of General Psychology	*Psychology Today*
Affiliated with the American Psychological Association	Published by Sussex Publishers
M. T. Pham's 2007 article: "Emotion and Rationality: A Critical Review and Interpretation of Empirical Evidence"	M. Hutson's 2015 article: "Beyond Happiness: The Upside of Feeling Down"

Internet Sources

Although internet sources provide a fascinating array of materials, some of the material posted on the internet has not been subjected to scholarly review and is, therefore, not necessarily credible. As a result, you should use only internet sources that meet important evaluative criteria.

- **Author, editor, host, or webmaster's credentials.** A website may or may not have an identified author, editor, host, or webmaster. If it does, however, explore the site for information about the webmaster's qualifications to discuss the topic.
- **Appropriate focus.** Skim the website to see whether its focus is suitable for your topic. Sometimes the site's title makes the focus clear; at other times, an entire site has a general focus, but its internal links allow you to locate material on narrower aspects of the larger subject.
- **Sufficient coverage.** Review documents on the website to see whether the coverage is thorough enough for your purposes.
- **Domains.** Examine the website's electronic address (URL) to see how the site is registered with the Internet Corporation for Assigned Names and Numbers (ICANN). The following common "top-level domains" provide useful clues about a site's focus and function.

   .com – A commercial site. The primary function of a commercial site is to make money.

   .edu – A site affiliated with an educational institution. These sites may be posted by the school or by an individual affiliated with the institution.

   .gov – A government site. These sites present trustworthy information (statistics, facts, reports), but the interpretive materials, if there are any, may be less useful.

   .mil – A military site. The technical information on these sites is consistently useful, but interpretive material tends to justify a single, pro-military position.

   .museum – A site for a museum. Because museums can be either nonprofit or for-profit institutions, consider the purpose that the particular museum serves.

   .org – An organizational site. Because organizations seek to advance political, social, financial, educational, and other specific agendas, review these materials with care.

- **Possible biases.** Do not automatically discount or overvalue what you find on any particular kind of website. Rather, consider the biases that influence how the information on a site is presented and interpreted.
- **Affiliation or sponsorship.** Examine the website to see whether it has an affiliation or a sponsorship beyond what is suggested by the site's domain.
- **Posting or revision date.** Identify the date of original posting or the date on which information was updated. Because currency is one of the benefits of internet sources, look for websites that provide recent information.
- **Documentation.** Review internet materials to see how thoroughly authors have documented their information. If facts, statistics, and other technical information are not documented appropriately, the information may be questionable.
- **Links to or from other sites.** Consider the "referral quality" that internet links provide.
- **Appropriate writing style.** Skim the website to see how it is written. All sources do not, of course, have to be written in the same style, but it is an issue worth considering when you evaluate a source.

Audiovisual Sources

Because of the range of audiovisual sources available, use specific criteria to assess each kind of source individually. Many of the techniques employed for evaluating these sources correspond to those used for print and internet sources.

- **Lectures and speeches.** Use criteria similar to those for print sources: speaker, relationship to your topic, coverage, sponsoring group or organization, and date.
- **Works of art, photographs, cartoons, and recordings.** Because these sources are used primarily to create interest in most research papers, consider how well the image or performance illuminates your topic.
- **Maps, graphs, tables, and charts.** Evaluate these visual sources the same way as you would evaluate traditional print sources.
- **Films, television shows, and radio programs.** When these sources serve informative purposes, evaluate them as you would assess print sources; when they are used creatively, evaluate them using the same criteria you would apply to other creative audiovisual forms.

Combinations of Sources

Although you must first evaluate your sources individually—whether they are print, internet, or audiovisual—your goal is to gather a set of high-quality sources that together provide a balanced treatment of your topic. Consider these issues.

- **Alternative perspectives.** Taken collectively, the work of your authors should provide a range of perspectives—academic and popular, liberal and conservative, theoretical and practical, current and traditional.

- **Different approaches to the topic.** Combine sources that range from the technical (including facts and statistics) to the interpretive (providing commentary and assessments). Also consider literature reviews for secondary analyses and empirical studies for primary research.

- **Diversity of sources.** Incorporate a wide range of sources—periodicals, books, electronic sources, and audiovisual sources—to ensure that you have taken advantage of the strengths of each kind of source. Be aware, however, that in some instances your research must focus on selected kinds of sources.

- **Varied publication, release, or distribution dates.** Include sources that represent the information, ideas, and interpretations of different periods, when appropriate.

Evaluating sources is an inexact process. No matter how carefully you review materials, some may later prove unhelpful. Yet early efforts to evaluate sources generally enhance the focus and efficiency of later, more comprehensive work, such as reading, taking notes, and, finally, writing the paper.

1f   Note-Taking

Note-taking is an individualized process: different researchers prefer different methods for recording information and ideas from sources. However, all note-taking should be meticulous and consistent, both to avoid plagiarism and to simplify the subsequent writing of the paper. Consider alternative methods for note-taking and remember that note-taking must be complete, consistent, matched to the kind of material being used, and honest.

Before taking notes from a source, create a complete and accurate entry for the reference list. See Chapters 4–8 for guidelines and samples.

Methods of Note-Taking

Begin your note-taking by analyzing each note-taking system and choosing the one best suited to your specific project, library facilities, work habits, and instructor's expectations.

- **Note cards.** Note cards are easy to handle and to rearrange during planning stages, but they hold only limited amounts of information.
- **Paper.** Paper is easy to handle and has sufficient room for copious notes, but notes on paper are difficult to organize during planning stages.
- **Computers.** Notes on computers do not have to be retyped during the writing process and can be printed multiple times, but on-site note-taking with computers is sometimes awkward.
- **Photocopies and printed texts.** Photocopied and printed materials do not have to be recopied, and you can write on them. However, photocopying and printing can be expensive.

Complete Information

Record complete identifying information with each separate note to avoid having to return to a source at a later, and potentially less convenient, time.

- **Author's name.** Record the author's last name (and first initial, if necessary for clarity); for multiauthor sources, record only as many names as are necessary for clarity.
- **Title.** Record only important words from titles but use italics or quotation marks as appropriate.
- **Category notation.** Provide a brief descriptive term to indicate the idea or subtopic that the information supports.
- **Page numbers.** Record the page number(s) from which you gathered information. If material comes from several pages, indicate where the page break occurs. (A double slash [//] is a useful way to indicate a page break.) Also indicate when an electronic source does not include pages.

Consistent Format

Record notes in a consistent format to avoid confusion at later stages of research and writing.

- **Placement of information.** Establish a consistent pattern for placing information so that nothing is omitted accidentally.
- **Abbreviations.** Use abbreviations selectively to save time and space; however, use only standard abbreviations to avoid possible confusion later.
- **Notations.** Note anything unique about the source (for example, no page numbers in a pamphlet or an especially good chart in an article).

Kinds of Notes

Four common kinds of notes serve most research purposes. Choose among these kinds of note-taking patterns depending on the sources and the kinds of materials they include.

- **Facts.** A fact note records technical information—names, dates, percentages—in minimal form. Record words, phrases, and information in a simple outline or list format and double-check the information for accuracy.
- **Summaries.** A summary note presents the substance of a passage in condensed form. After reading original material carefully, write a summary without looking at the original; this will ensure that the phrasing is yours, not the author's. Double-check the summary note to make sure that your wording is distinct from the original.
- **Paraphrases.** A paraphrase note restates ideas from a passage in your own words, using approximately the same number of words. Write a paraphrase without looking at the original and then double-check the note to ensure that the phrasing is yours.
- **Quotations.** A quotation note reproduces a writer's words exactly. Double-check the quotation note against the original; the copy must be an *exact* transcription of the original wording, capitalization, punctuation, and other elements.

Sample Note Card

- Author's name
- Category notation
- Paraphrased information
- A quoted phrase
- Pages

> Rohde   Family Stress
>
> – Family circumstances (fighting, negative activities, unreasonable demands) can make adolescent depression worse.
>
> – Family members must join in efforts to treat adolescent depression.
>
> – "At times the therapist who works with the adolescent must maintain an alliance both with the teenager and the parents in the face of conflict between the two."
>
> p. 24

Rohde, P. (2011). Cognitive behavior therapy treatment for adolescents. In D. W. Springer, A. Rubin, & C. G. Beevers (Eds.), *Treatment of depression in adolescents and adults* (pp. 21–27). Wiley.

1g Plagiarism

Plagiarism, from the Latin word for kidnapping, is the use of someone else's words, ideas, or line of thought without acknowledgment. In its most extreme form, plagiarism involves submitting someone else's completed work as your own. A less extreme but equally unacceptable form involves copying and pasting entire segments of another writer's work into your own writing. A third form of plagiarism involves carelessly or inadvertently blending elements (words, phrases, ideas) of a writer's work into your own.

- **Whole-paper plagiarism.** This kind of plagiarism is easily discovered. Through experiences with students in class, instructors learn what students are interested in and how they express themselves (sentence patterns, diction, and technical fluency).

- **Copy-and-paste plagiarism.** This kind of plagiarism is also easy to detect because of abrupt shifts in sentence sophistication, diction, or technical fluency.

- **Careless plagiarism.** This form of plagiarism is evident when distinct material is unquoted or when specialized information (dates, percentages, and other facts) is not acknowledged.

Even when this is carelessly or inadvertently done, the writer is still at fault for dishonest work, and the paper is still unacceptable.

Plagiarism can be easily detected by teachers and other readers when they note changes in vocabulary, sentence structure, and punctuation patterns or the inclusion of unexpected details, facts, and statistics. Moreover, current electronic means—either Google searches of key phrases or the reports of plagiarism software like Turnitin—quickly identify the sources of appropriated material.

In all of its forms, plagiarism is academically dishonest and unacceptable. Most colleges and universities now have specific plagiarism policies in place, and the penalties for its practice range from failing individual papers or projects to failing courses to being dismissed from college to having degrees revoked. The seriousness of plagiarism cannot be ignored, so you must make a conscious effort to avoid this practice. To avoid plagiarizing, learn to recognize the distinctive content and expression in source materials and take accurate, carefully punctuated, and documented notes.

Common Knowledge

Some kinds of information—facts and interpretations—are known by many people and are consequently described as common knowledge. That Alzheimer's disease is the leading cause of dementia in older adults is widely known, as is the more interpretive information that Alzheimer's disease is best treated by a combination of drug and psychiatric therapies. But common knowledge extends beyond these very general types of information to include more specific information within a field of study. In medical studies, for example, it is widely known that Prozac is the trade name for fluoxetine hydrochloride; in education, a commonly acknowledged interpretation is that high scores on standardized tests do not uniformly predict academic success. Documenting these facts, beliefs, and interpretations in a paper would be unnecessary because they are commonly known in their areas of study, even though you might have discovered them for the first time.

When you are researching an unfamiliar subject, distinguishing common knowledge that does not require documentation from special knowledge that does require documentation is sometimes difficult. The following guidelines may help.

What constitutes common knowledge

- **Historical facts** (names, dates, and general interpretations) that appear in many general reference books. For example, Sigmund Freud's most influential work, *The Interpretation of Dreams*, was published in 1899.
- **General observations and opinions** that are shared by many people. For example, it is a general observation that children learn by actively doing rather than passively listening, and it is a commonly held opinion that reading, writing, and arithmetic are the basic skills that elementary school students should acquire.
- **Unacknowledged information** that appears in multiple sources. For example, it is common knowledge that the earth's population is roughly 7.8 billion people and that an IQ is a gauge of intelligence determined by a person's knowledge in relation to his or her age.

If a piece of information does not meet these guidelines or if you are uncertain about whether it is common knowledge, always document the material.

Special Qualities of Source Materials

A more difficult problem than identifying common knowledge involves using an author's words and ideas improperly. Improper use often results from careless summarizing and paraphrasing. To use source materials without plagiarizing, learn to recognize their distinctive qualities.

Special qualities of sources

- **Distinctive prose style.** The author's chosen words, phrases, and sentence patterns.
- **Original facts.** Results of the author's personal research.
- **Personal interpretations of information.** The author's individual evaluation of his or her information.
- **Original ideas.** Ideas that are unique to a particular author.

As you work with sources, be aware of these distinguishing qualities and make certain that you do not incorporate into your writing the prose (word choices and sentence structures), original research, interpretations, or ideas of others without giving proper credit.

Consider, for example, the following paragraphs from Irvin Waller's (2011) *Rights for Victims of Crime: Rebalancing Justice* (Rowman).

Today, victims aren't the only ones who know about the pain, shock, humiliation, loss of control, and powerlessness that victims of crime experience at the hands of their offenders. A growing number of advocates and social scientists know only too well how feelings of anger, depression, worthlessness, and fear oscillate and reverberate over the weeks, months, years, and even decades following a victimizing incident. While law enforcement agents and judges may not be inclined to transfer their focus to the victim, many of these advocates and social scientists are experts in how to respond to victims in caring and just ways, and in some cases they even have solutions to stop victimization from happening in the future.

More often than not, we know how to provide emotional support and counseling to victims. We know how to protect the victim from the accused and how to give the victim a voice and power in the criminal justice system. We know how to inform victims of services that will help them and how to get them access to those services. We even know how to pay their mounting bills and how to stop much of the violence. In sum, we have the solutions as to how to put victims back in the center of our support, reparations, and justice systems. It's baffling, then, why governments are still not doing enough to apply this knowledge.

Now look at the following examples of faulty and acceptable summaries and paraphrases. Questionable phrases in the faulty samples are in red.

Faulty summary: plagiarism likely

> Waller   Advocates
>
> – People who support victims of violence understand that anger, depression, loss of self-worth, and worry last a long time following a victimizing incident.
>
> – Enforcement agents and judges aren't always inclined to focus on victims.
>
> p. 2

Acceptable summary: plagiarism unlikely

> **Waller** — Advocates
>
> - People who support victims of violence understand that "feelings of anger, depression, worthlessness, and fear oscillate and reverberate" long after a violent experience.
> - Victims aren't always the chief concern of those in the criminal justice system.
>
> p. 2

Faulty paraphrase: plagiarism likely

> **Waller** — What we know
>
> - We know how to give emotional support and counseling to support victims, how to protect victims and give them power in the justice system, how to help them find services and pay bills, and how to stop violence. In other words, we can make victims central in our support, payments, and justice system.
>
> p. 2

Acceptable paraphrase (see page 22)

1h Planning

After gathering information, organizing the research paper is an exciting stage because you are ready to bring ideas together in a clear and logical form.

Reviewing Notes

Begin by rereading the assignment sheet to reexamine the principles guiding your work. Then review your notes to see the range of materials you have collected and to identify connections among ideas.

Acceptable paraphrase: plagiarism unlikely

> Waller What we know
>
> – We know how to support victims emotionally and procedurally; we know how to protect them from future violence; we know how to ensure that they get the services they deserve. In other words, we already know how to make victims the focus of our efforts.
>
> p. 2

Thesis Statement, Hypothesis, or Stated Objective

After rereading your notes, revise the thesis statement, hypothesis, or objective so that it accurately represents the paper you plan to write. Is the topic clear? Does it express your current (more informed) view? Does it contain appropriate qualifications and limitations? Is it worded effectively?

Organization

Having reread your materials and reconsidered your thesis, hypothesis, or objective, plan the organization of your paper. Depending on the complexity of your paper, the requirements of your course, or your individual preferences, create either an informal outline (which is relatively simple and generally for your use only) or a formal outline (which is much more complex and generally intended for others). A complete discussion of both informal and formal outlines appears in Appendix C, Section C8.

Ii Writing Strategies

Because incorporating research materials and using in-text documentation extend the time it takes to write a paper, allow ample time to write the draft. Consider both the general and special circumstances that affect the process of writing and revising any paper, as well as those issues that relate specifically to writing and revising a documented paper.

General Strategies for Drafting a Paper

Because the research paper is in many ways like all other papers, keep these general writing strategies in mind.

- **Gather materials.** Collect planning materials and writing supplies before you begin writing. Working consistently in the same location is also helpful because all materials are there when you wish to write.
- **Work from an outline.** Following an outline (whether informal or formal), develop paragraphs and sections; write troublesome sections late in the process.
- **Keep the paper's purpose in mind.** Arrange and develop only those ideas that your outline indicates are important.
- **Develop the paper "promised" by the thesis, hypothesis, or objective.** Incorporate only the ideas and information that support your thesis, hypothesis, or objective.
- **Attend to technical matters later.** Concentrate on developing your ideas and presenting your information; you can revise the paper later to correct any technical errors.
- **Rethink troublesome sections.** When sections are difficult to write, reconsider their importance or means of development. Revise the outline if necessary.
- **Reread as you write.** Reread early sections as you write to maintain a consistent tone and style.
- **Write alternative sections.** Write several versions of troublesome sections and then choose the best one.
- **Take periodic breaks.** Get away from your work for short periods so that you can maintain a fresh perspective and attain objectivity.

Strategies for Drafting a Research Paper

Because the research paper has its own distinct qualities and demands, keep these special strategies in mind.

- **Allow ample time.** Give yourself plenty of time to write a research paper; its length and complexity will affect the speed at which you work.
- **Think about sections, not paragraphs.** Think of the paper in terms of sections, not paragraphs. Large sections will probably contain several paragraphs.

- **Use transitions.** Although headings can divide your work into logical segments, use well-chosen transitional words to signal shifts between elements of the paper.
- **Attend to technical language.** Define technical terms carefully to clarify ideas.
- **Incorporate notes smoothly.** Use research materials to support and illustrate, not dominate, your discussion.
- **Document carefully.** Use parenthetical citations to acknowledge the sources of your ideas and information (see Chapter 4, "Preparing the Reference List and Parenthetical Citations").

Questions for Revising Content

Examine the paper's content for clarity, coherence, and completeness. Consider these issues.

- **Title, introduction, headings, conclusion.** Are your title, introduction, headings, and conclusion well matched to the tone and purpose of the paper?
- **Thesis, hypothesis, or stated objective and development.** Does the thesis accurately represent your current view on the topic, and does the paper develop that idea? Does your paper develop in response to your hypothesis? Is the content of your paper matched to your stated objective?
- **Support for thesis, hypothesis, or stated objective.** Do research materials effectively support the paper's thesis, hypothesis, or stated objective? Have you eliminated materials (details, sentences, even paragraphs) that do not directly support your thesis, hypothesis, or stated objective?
- **Organization.** Does your organizational pattern present your ideas logically and effectively?
- **Use of materials.** Have you incorporated a range of materials to develop your ideas in a varied, interesting, and complete way?
- **Balance among sections.** Are the sections of the paper balanced in length and emphasis?
- **Balance among sources.** Have you used a variety of sources to support your ideas?
- **Transitions.** Do transitions connect sections of the paper in a coherent way?

Questions for Revising Style

Achieving coherent, balanced, well-developed content is one aspect of revision. Another consideration is achieving a clear and compelling presentation. Refine the paper's style, keeping these issues in mind.

- **Tone.** Is the tone suited to the topic and presentation?
- **Sentences.** Are the sentences varied in both length and type? Have you written active, rather than passive, sentences?
- **Diction.** Are the word choices vivid, accurate, and appropriate?
- **Introduction of research materials.** Have you introduced research materials (facts, summaries, paraphrases, and quotations) with variety and clarity?

Questions for Revising Technical Matters

Technical revision focuses on grammar, usage, punctuation, mechanics, spelling, and manuscript form. After revising content and style, consider technical revisions to make the presentation correct and precise, giving particular attention to issues related to documentation.

- **Grammar.** Are your sentences complete? Do pronouns agree in number and gender with their antecedents? Do verbs agree with their subjects? Have you worked to avoid errors that you commonly make? (Appendix C includes discussions of seven common technical problems.)
- **Punctuation and mechanics.** Have you double-checked your punctuation? Have you spell-checked the paper? Have you used quotation marks and italics correctly?
- **Quotations.** Are quotations presented correctly, depending on their length or emphasis?
- **Parenthetical citations.** Are parenthetical citations placed appropriately and punctuated correctly?
- **Reference list.** Have you listed only the sources actually used in the paper? Is your list alphabetized correctly? Is each entry complete and correct?
- **Manuscript guidelines.** Are margins, line spacing, and paging correct? Does the paper include all necessary elements?

2 Preparing APA Manuscripts

Chapter Objectives:

- Learn the parts of an APA manuscript.
- Learn how to create each part of the manuscript.
- Become familiar with general manuscript guidelines.

APA style guidelines for manuscript preparation ensure that manuscripts follow uniform standards and, as a result, present the elements of papers in a generally understood way.

2a Parts of the Manuscript

A manuscript for an APA paper can contain as many as eight separate parts: the title page (with author note), an abstract (with keywords), the text of the paper, a list of references, footnotes, tables, figures, and appendices. Not all papers have all of these elements, but when they do, they are arranged in this order.

Instructors often vary their manuscript requirements depending on the course or circumstance. Papers for lower-division courses may require only the most basic elements (title page, text, and references) and follow APA's simplified manuscript guidelines for students (for example, no running head or abstract). However, papers for upper-division and graduate courses may require all elements of an APA manuscript and follow professional standards for manuscript preparation. Consequently, you need to review course requirements carefully. (See Chapter 9 for samples of both formats.)

The first part of this chapter addresses the specific requirements for preparing each element of an APA paper. The last part provides general manuscript guidelines.

Title Page

The first page of a manuscript is the title page (see pages 115, 126, and 127 for samples), composed of the following elements.

- **Running head with paging.** As the first line of the title page, supply a running head—a shortened version of the paper's title typed in all capital letters—with the page number. Full instructions for creating the running head appear on page 38, and samples appear on pages 115 and 127.

- **Title.** Three lines below the running head, center the title (in boldface type) and use headline-style capitalization (see pages 50 and 51). A good title is descriptive, clarifying both the topic and the perspective of the paper; when possible, the title should also create interest through effective wording. If the title is longer than one line, divide it logically and center both lines.
- **Author's name.** Four lines below the title, type your name (centered and capitalized normally); APA recommends using your first name and middle initial(s) for additional clarity. Two lines below your name, identify your affiliation; typically, this is your school's name, but you can indicate the city and state where you live. (Alternately, you can provide, on four separate lines, your name, the course name and number, the instructor's name, and the submission date.)
- **Author note.** At least four spaces below the affiliation, type the phrase *Author Note* (centered, in boldface type, but not italicized), followed by a series of clarifying paragraphs: (a) the first paragraph identifies the author's Open Researcher and Contributor Identification number (ORCID iD number); (b) the second paragraph identifies changes in affiliation, if any; (c) the third paragraph includes any necessary disclaimers, disclosures, or explanations of special circumstances, followed by acknowledgments; and (d) the fourth paragraph presents the author's contact information. Use separate, indented, double-spaced paragraphs for each element.

NOTE: An author note is not typically required for student work: papers for classes, theses, and dissertations.

Parts of an APA Paper

- **Title page.** The opening page incorporates information to label the pages of the paper, highlights the title of the paper, and provides identifying information about the author. An author note may be included at the bottom of the title page.
- **Abstract.** This paragraph presents a brief but detailed overview of the paper, emphasizing key ideas and research procedures.
- **Text.** The text of an argumentative paper or review contains an introduction, body, and conclusion; it is frequently divided using headings that describe the

main elements of the discussion. The text of a research study contains an introduction to the topic or problem (including a literature review), an explanation of methodology, a summary of results, and a discussion of the implications of the study.

- **Reference list.** The alphabetically arranged reference list provides publication information for the sources used in the paper.
- **Footnotes.** Content footnotes include clarifying discussions and explanations that might disrupt the flow of the paper. Alternatively, footnotes may be incorporated within the text of the paper using the footnote function of your word processor.
- **Tables.** Numbered tables include technical data in easily interpreted and comparable forms. References within the paper correspond to tables which may appear on separate pages near the end of the manuscript or in the text of the paper.
- **Figures.** Visual images to support ideas in a paper (drawings, graphs, photographs, maps, and so on) appear as numbered figures. References within the paper correspond to the figures which may appear on separate pages at the end of the manuscript or in the text of the paper.
- **Appendices.** Appendices provide supplementary information that supports the ideas in the paper but would be awkward to include in the paper itself.

Abstract

The abstract (the second page of the manuscript) follows the title page and provides a brief description of the major ideas in the paper (see pages 115 and 127 for samples). Because it must summarize the full range of ideas and information in the paper, an abstract is generally written after the manuscript is complete. It must adhere to the following guidelines.

- **Heading.** Three lines below the running head, type the word *Abstract*, centered, in boldface type, but not italicized. Two lines below, begin the paragraph.
- **Format.** The abstract is a single, unindented, double-spaced paragraph.

- **Length.** Abstracts in APA journals are typically no more than 250 words.
- **Concision.** To save space in the abstract, you may use standard abbreviations (for example, *AMA* rather than *American Medical Association*); use digits for all numbers except those that begin sentences; and use active, rather than passive, voice. (See Appendix C, section C6.)
- **Content.** In the opening sentence, describe the topic or problem addressed in the paper. Use the remaining words in the paragraph to clarify methodology (for a research study), to identify four or five major ideas, and to explain results or conclusions. If a paper is lengthy and multifaceted, describe only the most important elements.
- **Keywords.** You may include a list of keywords with your abstract. Two lines below the abstract, indent, type *Keywords* (italicized, followed by a colon), and provide three to five words (not italicized) that best describe the content of your paper (see page 127 for a sample).

Text

The text of the paper begins on the third page of the manuscript (see pages 116–122 and 128–133 for sample pages). The running head, as always, appears on the top line. Three lines below, center the title, with headline-style capitalization, in boldface type, but without other print features (italics, underlining, change in font size, or quotation marks). Two lines below the title, the double-spaced paper begins. The organization of the body of the paper depends on the paper's focus.

An Argumentative Paper, Review, or Meta-Analysis

- **Introduction.** Define, describe, or clarify the topic (problem) and place it within its historical or scholarly context. Present a thesis (a statement of your topic and opinion) to clarify the purpose of your work.
- **Body.** Examine the facets of the topic (problem) by reviewing current research: evaluate the positions held by others; analyze current data; assess the interpretations of others; synthesize the information and ideas found in other people's work. Use headings and subheadings throughout this section to direct readers through your argument.
- **Conclusion.** Summarize key points, draw connections among important ideas, and reiterate your thesis.

- **Reference list.** In this labeled section, provide a list of sources cited in the paper (see Chapter 4).
- **Additional materials.** As appropriate, include the following labeled sections: footnotes, tables, figures, and appendices.

A Research Study

- **Introduction.** In this unlabeled section, describe the problem, state your hypothesis, and describe your research methodology. Consider the importance of the problem and the ways in which the study addresses the problem. Present a historical or contextual discussion of what scholars have written, acknowledging alternative perspectives and differing interpretations.
- **Method.** In this labeled section (further divided into labeled subsections), describe participants in the study (and procedures for selecting them), materials used (ranging from standard equipment to custom materials), and procedures (the step-by-step process for conducting the research).
- **Results.** In this labeled section, summarize the gathered information. It should be further subdivided into labeled subsections that analyze information that is illustrated by tables, figures, and other statistical material.
- **Discussion.** In this labeled section, make an assertion about the correlation of your data with your original hypothesis. The remaining discussion can address how your findings relate to the work of others, what qualifications are necessary, the value of alternative interpretations, or what conclusions you have reached. End the discussion by commenting on the significance of your research results.
- **Reference list.** In this labeled section, provide a list of sources cited in the paper (see Chapter 4).
- **Additional materials.** As appropriate, include the following labeled sections: footnotes, tables, figures, and appendices.

Reference List

The reference list, which continues the paging of the entire manuscript, provides publishing information for all sources used in the paper (see pages 123 and 134 for samples). Chapter 4 provides a comprehensive discussion of the information required in reference-list entries and the format for presenting the information. Chapters 5 through 8 provide explanations of 56 kinds of sources, with 114 separate samples for preparing reference-list entries for periodicals, books and other print materials, audiovisual sources, and electronic sources. Each entry appears with a corresponding parenthetical citation.

2b Footnotes

Content footnotes allow writers to provide additional discussion or clarification that, although important, might disrupt the flow of a paper.

Footnotes follow these guidelines for placement and presentation.

- **Heading.** Three lines below the running head, type the word *Footnotes*, centered, in boldface type, but not italicized.
- **Order of notes.** On the footnote page, footnotes appear in the order in which references appear in the text of the paper. Double-check the numbering.
- **Format.** Footnotes are typed in paragraph style, double-spaced, with the first line indented and subsequent lines aligned at the left margin. "Tab" once (for a five-space indentation), insert the superscript number, and type the footnote. No space separates the note number from the first letter of the first word of the footnote.
- **Paging.** Footnotes appear on a new page. Multiple footnotes are placed on the same page, with no additional space between the notes.

NOTE: You may also incorporate footnotes within the text of the paper using the footnote function of your word-processing program.

Placing Note Numbers in the Paper

- **In-text notes.** Footnotes are numbered sequentially throughout a paper.
- **Placement of in-text note numbers.** In the text of the paper, refer to a content note by using a superscript number (a number placed above the line, like this[1]) without additional space. Word-processing programs allow you to achieve this result in multiple ways: using the superscript icon on the toolbar, using the superscript option under the "Font" feature, or using the "Insert" feature to place a footnote.
- **Punctuation and note numbers.** Note numbers follow all punctuation marks, except dashes and parentheses.

A note number precedes the dash[2]—without additional space. A note number may appear within parentheses (when it refers only to materials within the parentheses[3]). If the note refers to the entire sentence, however, it follows the parentheses (as in this sample).[4]

Tables

Because tables present labeled information in columns (vertical elements) and rows (horizontal elements) for easy interpretation or comparison, they are helpful additions to papers that use technical data (see page 137 for a sample). Within the text of the paper, a reference (for example, "See Table 1") directs readers to tables using numerals (which correspond to tables presented near the end of the manuscript). Tables are often prepared on separate pages and are presented according to these principles.

- **Table identification.** Three lines below the running head (flush with the left margin), type the word *Table* and the table's Arabic numeral (Table 3, Table 4), in boldface type but not italicized.
- **Title of the table.** Two spaces below the table identification, also flush left, type the title of the table in italics, with headline-style capitalization. One line below, insert a horizontal, 1-point rule (line); use the graphics or "Insert" feature of your word-processing program to create this element.
- **Column headings.** Use sentence-style capitalization for column headings and center the column heading over the information in each column. One line below the column headings, insert a horizontal rule.
- **Parallel information and style.** To maintain consistency, headings should appear in parallel grammatical forms (all nouns, all gerunds, and so on), and numbers should appear in similar style (with decimals, rounded to whole numbers, and so on).
- **Spacing.** The primary elements of tables may be single-spaced, one-and-a-half spaced, or double-spaced; columns should be separated by at least three spaces for visual clarity. However, table notes (general and specific) are always double-spaced.
- **Repeated information.** If information from a table extends beyond one page, repeat the column headings.
- **Table notes (general).** To provide an explanation of an entire table, include a general note. One line below the body of the table, insert a horizontal rule. Two lines below the rule, type the word *Note* (italicized and flush with the left margin)

followed by a period; after one space, type the text of the note, which remains flush left if it extends beyond one line. Place a period at the end of the note, even if it is not a complete sentence. General notes are double-spaced.

- **Table notes (specific).** To provide an explanation of a specific element within a table, include a specific note. Within the table, insert a superscript lowercase letter—like this[a]— following the element. One line below the body of the table, insert a horizontal rule. Below the horizontal rule and flush with the left margin, insert the corresponding superscript lowercase letter, followed by the explanation. Place a period at the end of the note, even if it is not a complete sentence. If a table also has a general table note, it appears first; the specific table note appears on the line below. If a table has two or more specific notes, they continue on the same line, separated by one space. Specific table notes are double-spaced.

- **Formatting.** Avoid the decorative formatting that word-processing programs include among table options—with shading, grid formats, and other decorative features. Instead, use only the horizontal rules that begin and end a table and use space to separate columns visually.

- **Paging.** Each table must begin on a new page.

NOTE: You can also incorporate tables within the text of the paper. Refer to them in your text (use phrases like "as noted in Table 1" or "See Table 1") and place the tables as close as possible to the discussion that they illustrate.

Figures

Figures are visual elements—drawings, graphs, photographs, maps, and so on—that cannot be reproduced by traditional typing (see page 137 for a sample). Each figure is numbered as it is used in the paper; original figures then appear on separate pages at the end of the manuscript, following these guidelines.

- **Figure identification.** Three lines below the running head (flush with the left margin), type the word *Figure* and the figure's Arabic number (Figure 2, Figure 3) in boldface type, not italicized.

- **Title.** Two spaces below the figure identification, also flush left, type the title of the figure in italics, with headline-style capitalization.

- **Figure.** Two lines below the title, insert the figure in the highest quality possible, with sharp contrast in photographs, distinct shading in bar graphs, and clear lettering in line graphs. Figures must be scaled to fit appropriately on the page.

- **Figure note.** Clarify or highlight elements of a figure by providing a figure note. Two lines below the figure, type the word *Note* (italicized and flush with the left margin), followed by a period. After one space, include your explanation (double-spaced).
- **Spacing and indentation.** Figure notes are double-spaced. If a note extends beyond one line, it continues flush left.
- **Fonts.** Printed text that is part of a figure—labels, for example—should use a sans-serif font such as Calibri. The minimum acceptable font size is 8 points, with 14 points being the maximum.
- **Paging.** Each figure must be presented on a separate page.

NOTE: You can also incorporate figures within the text of the paper. Refer to them in your text (use phrases like "as noted in Figure 2" or "See Figure 3") and place the figures as close as possible to the discussion that they illustrate.

Special Concerns for Figures

- **Value of the figure.** Consider whether the figure presents information more effectively than would a textual discussion or a table. Because figures are more difficult to prepare than print-based elements, make sure that your time is well spent in creating one.
- **Computer-generated figures.** Today's word-processing programs are capable of creating a wide range of figures, including bar graphs, line graphs, and pie charts. Allow sufficient time to familiarize yourself with the procedures for creating a figure.
- **Visual clutter.** Include only figures that highlight important elements of your discussion. To achieve this goal, eliminate all extraneous detail in graphs, charts, and drawings and crop (trim) photographs and maps to focus visual attention on key features, not superficial or unrelated elements.
- **Visual clarity.** To ensure that figures achieve maximum impact, make sure that the print quality of graphs and charts is high (best achieved by laser printing). Furthermore, make sure that bar charts, photographs, and maps are sharply focused and have clear tonal contrast.

Appendices

One or more appendices can follow figures and continue the page numbering of the entire manuscript (see page 138 for a sample). Each appendix should adhere to the following guidelines.

- **Heading.** Three lines below the running head, type the word *Appendix*, centered, in boldface type, but not italicized. If more than one appendix is included, label each one with a letter (Appendix A, Appendix B).
- **Appendix title.** Two lines below the heading, type the title of the appendix, centered, with boldface type and headline-style capitalization.
- **Text.** Begin the text two lines below the appendix title; appended material is double-spaced.
- **Paging.** Each appendix begins on a new page.

2c General Manuscript Guidelines

In preparing a paper in APA style, writers must conform to a variety of principles, each of which is described in the following sections.

Paper

Use heavy-weight, white bond, 8½″ × 11″ paper. Avoid lightweight paper because it does not hold up well under review or grading.

Font Selection

Fonts—designed versions of letters, numbers, and characters—appear in different sizes, referred to as *points*. APA no longer restricts font selection, as long as the same font is used throughout the text of the paper. Serif fonts (those with cross marks on individual letters) are the traditional choices—including Book Antiqua, Garamond, Times, Times New Roman, and others. Sans serif fonts (those without cross marks) provide other options—including Arial, Calibri, Tahoma, and others. Whichever font you choose, the point size must be 10–12 points for the primary text.

NOTE: Labels within figures must be in san serif fonts; the size can range from 8–14 points.

Use italics (*slanted type*), not underlining, in all parts of your paper. Use your word-processing program's capabilities to insert accents, diacritical marks, and symbols directly in your paper, rather than adding them by hand.

Font Sizes, Fonts, and Their Uses

FONT SIZE	SERIF	SANS-SERIF	USES
8 pt.		Tahoma	Figures
12 pt.	Times New Roman		Primary text and supporting materials
14 pt.		Century Gothic	Figures

Line Spacing

Double-space all parts of the paper except some supporting elements: tables and figures may use different line spacing to enhance clarity, footnotes that are incorporated into the paper may be single-spaced, and equations and other visual elements can be set off with triple- or quadruple-spacing.

NOTE: Three lines separate the running head from the elements of the paper.

Word Spacing

Use one space after end punctuation (periods, question marks, and exclamation points), internal punctuation (commas, colons, and semicolons), periods with initials (E. V. Debbs), and between elements in citations. No space is required with periods in abbreviations (p.m., e.g., U.S.), with hyphens (first-year student), or with dashes (example: The sounds of vowels—*a, e, i, o, u*—must be transcribed carefully to record speech accurately).

Margins and Indentations

Leave 1-inch margins at the left, right, top, and bottom of each page. If the "default" margins for your word-processing program are not 1 inch, reset them to 1 inch. Do not justify the right margin (that is, create a straight text edge on the right); instead, use left justification, which aligns the text on the left but leaves the right margin irregular (ragged). Do not hyphenate words at the ends of lines.

A five- to seven-space indentation (½ inch)—best achieved by using the "Tab" feature—is required at the beginning of paragraphs and for the first line of footnotes. The continuous indentation that is required for long quotations and for second and subsequent lines of reference-list entries is best achieved by using the "Indent" feature.

Seriation

To indicate a series or a sequence within a prose paragraph, enclose lowercase letters in parentheses. Although this pattern should not be overused, it has two advantages: (a) It provides visual clarity, and (b) it makes a long sentence with multiple elements easily readable. To achieve a similar effect with a series of set-off sentences or paragraphs, use Arabic numerals followed by periods.

1. Indent the number five to seven spaces from the margin (½ inch).
2. After a period and one space, type the word, phrase, sentence, or paragraph.
3. If the item continues beyond one line, subsequent lines can be flush left or indented.

When elements are not presented in chronological order or by order of importance, they may be set off using bullets (typically filled circles or squares).

- This pattern draws attention to each element.
- The order of elements is deemphasized.
- Indentation patterns are the same as for numbered lists.

Paging (Running Head)

On the first line of the title page, flush left, type an abbreviated version of the title of the paper in all capital letters; it can contain no more than 50 characters (letters, numbers, symbols, punctuation, and spaces). On the same line, flush right, insert the page number. This information (abbreviated title and page number) must be at least one-half inch from the top of the page; the text begins three lines below the running head (see pages 115 and 127 for samples).

Use the "Header" feature of your word-processing program to type the running head and use codes to insert page numbers automatically throughout the document.

NOTE: Student papers do not have to include a running head. Instead, insert the page number only, flush right.

Headings for Sections

Use headings to divide and subdivide the paper into logical, and sometimes sequential, sections. APA establishes five potential levels of division for manuscripts, while acknowledging that most writing does not require the use of all five.

- **Level-1 headings** are centered, with headline-style capitalization and boldface type. The text follows two lines below.
- **Level-2 headings** are flush left, with headline-style capitalization and boldface type. The text follows two lines below.
- **Level-3 headings** are flush left, with headline-style capitalization, and boldface italic type. The text follows two lines below.
- **Level-4 headings** are indented, with headline-style capitalization, boldface type, and a period. After one space, the text follows on the same line.
- **Level-5 headings** are indented, with headline-style capitalization, boldface italic type, and a period. After one space, the text follows on the same line.

One level of division

> **Level-1 Heading**

Two levels of division

> **Level-1 Heading**
>
> **Level-2 Heading**

Three levels of division

> **Level-1 Heading**
>
> **Level-2 Heading**
>
> ***Level-3 Heading***

Four levels of division

> **Level-1 Heading**
>
> **Level-2 Heading**
>
> ***Level-3 Heading***
>
>   **Level-4 Heading.**

Five levels of division

> **Level-1 Heading**
>
> **Level-2 Heading**
>
> ***Level-3 Heading***
>
>   **Level-4 Heading.**
>
>   ***Level-5 Heading.***

When new headings are required, do not begin new pages. Simply type the new heading two lines below the last line of the preceding paragraph.

Submitting the Paper

Submit manuscripts according to your instructor's guidelines, acknowledging that alternative formats and methods exist.

- **Paper submission.** Staple the pages in the upper-left corner. Some instructors accept the paper only; others ask that the paper be placed in a manila envelope with your name and affiliation typed or written on the outside; yet others ask that the paper be submitted in a folder. Whichever pattern your instructor requires, always save a copy of the file on your computer.
- **Electronic submission.** Submit the paper through an electronic service like Turnitin. Such services allow you to upload your paper through a link created by your instructor. After you have uploaded the paper, preview it to ensure that you have uploaded the correct version and, very importantly, "confirm" the submission—a step that finalizes the process and makes the paper available to your instructor. You will receive an email confirmation if the paper has been successfully submitted; print a copy of the confirmation email for your records.
- **Email submission.** Attach the file version of the paper to an email with a clear subject line (Paper 4: Test Anxiety), as well as a note about the word-processing program you used. If you do not receive confirmation of delivery, resubmit the email and attachment. Print a copy of your email as a record.
- **Flash drive submission.** Submit a copy of the final paper on a flash drive, clearly labeled with your name and affiliation, as well as a note about the word-processing program you used. Save a copy of the file on your computer.

3 Following APA Editorial Style

Chapter Objectives:

- Learn APA patterns for using punctuation.
- Learn APA standards for using mechanics (quotation marks, capitalization, italics, and number style).
- Learn effective ways to use transitions, verb tense, agreement, and parallelism.
- Learn about effective word choice.

Generally, APA style follows conventions that need little explanation (for example, periods follow sentences that make statements, and question marks follow sentences that pose questions). However, in some situations, agreement about editorial issues is not universal. (Should commas separate *all* elements of listed items? Are prepositions in titles capitalized?) In such special circumstances, follow the APA guidelines in this chapter to ensure that your manuscript meets expectations.

3a Punctuation and Mechanics

Periods

Periods most often serve as end punctuation (after sentences), but they are also used with abbreviations and in other specialized contexts.

USES OF PERIODS	EXAMPLES
End of a complete sentence	Periods end most sentences.
Initials with an author's name	C. S. Lewis
Reference-list abbreviations	Ed., Vol. 6, pp. 34–38, Rev. ed.
Table and figure notes	*Note.* Student use of computers.
Latin abbreviations	i.e., e.g., vs., p.m.
U.S. when used as an adjective	U.S. government, U.S. economy
Abbreviation for inch	in. (distinct from the preposition *in*)
Decimal points in fractions	2.45 ml, 33.5 lb

SPECIAL CASES—NO PERIODS	EXAMPLES
Abbreviations for states, provinces, and territories	AZ (Arizona), IL (Illinois), BC (British Columbia), PR (Puerto Rico)
Acronyms (shortened forms of multiword names using first letters)	APA (American Psychological Association), FBI (Federal Bureau of Investigation), ER (emergency room)
After DOIs or URLs (at the end of reference-list entries)	Miller, G. (2010, May). How our brains make memories. *Smithsonian*, 41(2), 38–45. https://smithsonianmag.com/science-nature/how-our-brains-make-memories-14466850/

Commas

Commas are internal forms of punctuation, most often used to separate elements within sentences. However, they also serve a few other purposes.

USES OF COMMAS	EXAMPLES
Three or more items in a series	Men, women, and children
Set off nonessential information	The room, which was well lighted, was on the south corridor.
Clauses of a compound sentence	The first survey was a failure, but the second one was a success.
Years with exact dates	May 25, 2019, the experiment began. *But* May 2019, the experiment began.
Years within parenthetical citations	(Armstrong, 2020); (Romines, 2017)
Numbers of 1,000 or larger	11,205 students, 1,934 books (see "Commas in Numbers," page 54, for exceptions)

Semicolons

In APA style, semicolons serve four purposes, all related to separating elements for which confusion is possible.

USES OF SEMICOLONS	EXAMPLES
Join clauses of a compound sentence when no coordinating conjunction is used	Females responded positively; males responded negatively.
Join clauses of a compound sentence when a conjunctive adverb (*however, furthermore*) is used	Stress manifests itself in a variety of subtle ways; however, trained clinicians can recognize behaviors and provide assistance.
Separate multiple sources within the same parenthetical citation	(Edwards, 2018; Elkins, 2017)
Separate elements in a series when the elements contain commas	The test groups were from Fresno, California; St. Louis, Missouri; and Raleigh, North Carolina.

Colons

Colons serve four distinct purposes in APA style. A complete sentence must precede the colon, and if the explanatory material that follows a colon is a complete sentence, the first word is capitalized.

USES OF COLONS	EXAMPLES
Introduce a phrase that serves as an explanation or illustration	Two words triggered the strongest reactions: *preferential* and *special*.
Introduce a sentence that serves as an explanation or illustration (the first word of the clarifying sentence is capitalized)	The responses were quickly summarized: Patients were dissatisfied.
Separate the title from the subtitle (the first word of the subtitle is capitalized)	*Decoding delinquency: Psychological and social factors that influence youth behavior* (This sample is capitalized as it would appear in the reference list.)
Separate elements in a ratio	The ratio was 3:10.

Dashes

Formed by typing two hyphens (with no spaces before and after) or using the em-dash feature of your word-processing program, dashes serve a few selected purposes; however, they should be used sparingly in academic writing. Also note that if a title contains a dash, the word that follows the dash is capitalized.

USES OF DASHES	EXAMPLES
Indicate a break in the thought of the sentence	The national heritage of participants—they identified themselves—proved less important than researchers anticipated.
Insert a series of elements that contain commas	Universities in two small cities—Terre Haute, Indiana, and Bloomington, Illinois—offer similar programs in psychology.

The shorter and more specialized en dash, which can be inserted using your word-processing program, is used to indicate inclusive pages in reference-list entries and parenthetical citations (pp. 102–133, pp. 435–436) and to show equal weight in a compound modifier (parent–teacher conference, doctor–patient relationship).

Hyphens

Hyphens are most often used to join compound words that precede the noun they modify; this pattern ensures that modification is clear in individual sentences (example: First-person narratives are seldom suitable in academic writing). When the modifiers follow the noun, they are generally written without hyphens (example: The opening paragraph was written in the first person). When general usage determines that a compound has become a permanent part of the language, it may be spelled either open (high school) or closed (casebook); consult a collegiate dictionary for individual cases.

USES OF HYPHENS	EXAMPLES
A compound that functions as an adjective	high-risk behaviors, time-intensive work, all-or-nothing approach

continued on next page

Punctuation and Mechanics   3a

USES OF HYPHENS	EXAMPLES
A compound with a number that functions as an adjective	two-part explanation, sixth-grade teacher, 50-word paragraph
A compound using the prefix *self-*	self-help books, self-inflicted injuries, self-imposed limitations
A compound that could be misread	re-form ("form again," not "change"), re-mark ("mark again," not "comment"), re-count ("count again," not "remember")
A compound using a prefix when the base word is capitalized	anti-American sentiment, pseudo-Freudian interpretation, post-Depression regulations
A compound using a prefix when the base word is a number	pre-1960s complacency, post-2010 requirements
A compound using a prefix when the base word is more than one word	non-user-friendly instructions, pro-distance-education initiative, non-peer-reviewed journals
A fraction used as an adjective	three-fourths majority
A prefix that ends with the first letter of the base word (except e)	anti-inflammatory drug, post-traumatic stress (but preexisting condition)

SPECIAL CASES—NO HYPHENATION	EXAMPLES
A compound with an adverb ending in *-ly*	newly designed test, recently certified teacher, uncharacteristically exaggerated statement
A compound with a comparative or superlative adjective	less capable practitioner, clearer written instructions, most egregious error
A foreign phrase used as a modifier	ad hoc committee, a priori reasoning, laissez faire attitude

continued on next page

SPECIAL CASES—NO HYPHENATION	EXAMPLES
A common fraction used as a noun	two thirds of students, one half of the sample, one quarter of the residents
A modifier that uses a letter or number to represent a sequence	Table C placement, Type I error, Step 1 explanation

Quotation Marks

Quotation marks are used within the text of a paper to identify titles of brief works, to indicate a quotation containing fewer than 40 words, and to highlight words used in special ways.

NOTE: Quotation marks are not used in reference-list entries, and quotations of more than 40 words are indented and use no quotation marks. (See Section 4f for additional information on quoted material.)

USES OF QUOTATION MARKS	EXAMPLES
Titles of chapters, articles, songs, and so on (quotation marks are used in the text only; reference-list entries *do not* use quotation marks)	"The High-Risk Child" (chapter), "Grant Writing vs. Grant Getting" (article), "My Vietnam" (song)
Quoted material (written or spoken) of fewer than 40 words when used word for word	Duncan (2019) asserted, "Normative behavior is difficult to define because community standards apply" (p. 233).
Words used counter to their intended meaning (irony, slang, or coined usage)	Her "abnormal" behavior was, in fact, quite normal.
Words or letters that are linguistically identified as words or letters (Alternately, they can be italicized; see page 51.)	Different impressions are created by the words "small," "diminutive," "minute," and "tiny."

Parentheses

Parentheses are used, always in pairs, to separate information and elements from the rest of the sentence.

USES OF PARENTHESES	EXAMPLES
Set off clarifying information	We provided parents with four samples (see Figures 1–4).
Set off publication dates in in-text summaries	Wagner (2017) noted that special-needs students responded well to the protocol.
Set off parenthetical citations within the text; they must correspond to entries in the reference list	First-time offenders are more likely to respond to group therapy sessions than are repeat offenders (Gillum & Sparks, 2019).
Set off page references that follow direct quotations	Sanchez (2018) noted, "Self-concept is an intangible quality among immigrant children" (p. 34).
Introduce an abbreviation to be used in place of a full name in subsequent sections of a paper	The American Psychological Association (APA) published its first guidelines for manuscript preparation in 1929. Since then, APA has updated its guidelines nine times.
Set off letters that indicate divisions or sequences within paragraphs	The test included sections on (a) vocabulary, (b) reading comprehension, and (c) inferences.

Brackets

Brackets are used within parentheses or quotation marks to provide clarifying information. Use brackets sparingly because they can become distracting in academic writing.

USES OF BRACKETS	EXAMPLES
Clarifying information in a quotation	Thompson (2016) observed, "When [students] work in groups, they perform better" (p. 11). (Used to replace *they* in the original text.)
Parenthetical information already in parentheses	(See Figure 4 [Percentages of students with learning disabilities] for more details.)

continued on next page

USES OF BRACKETS	EXAMPLES
Clarifying information in a reference-list entry	*Eternal sunshine of the spotless mind* [film].
Indicate an editorial note	Bailey (2019) noted that "family members *and* [italics mine] friends must agree to support a patient's recovery plan" (p. 219).

Slashes

Slashes serve very specialized functions, often related to the presentation of compounds, comparisons, and correlations.

USES OF SLASHES	EXAMPLES
Hyphenated compounds in alternatives	first-day/second-day experiences
Fractions (numerator/denominator)	3/4, X + Y/Z
Represent *per* in units with a numerical value	0.7 ml/L
Indicate phonemes in English	/b/
Separate dual publication dates for reprinted works	Hirsch (1999/2009)

Capitalization

APA follows universally accepted patterns for most capitalization. However, APA uses two distinct capitalization patterns for titles—headline style and sentence style (also referred to as headline case and sentence case)—depending on whether they appear in the text of the paper or in the reference list.

USES OF CAPITALIZATION	EXAMPLES
Proper nouns and proper adjectives	Jean Piaget, Robert Coles, Chinese students, Elizabethan drama
Specific departments (and academic units) in universities and specific courses	Department of Psychology, Indiana State University, Criminology 235

continued on next page

USES OF CAPITALIZATION	EXAMPLES
Job or position titles before a name (but not after or if used in a general sense)	President Obama, Dr. Harper Sloane, Judge Jeremy Alcott
Names for racial or ethnic groups	Black, Hispanic, Muslim, Christian
Trade and brand names	Prozac, Xerox, WordPerfect X9
Titles of articles or parts of books in the text: Use headline-style capitalization.	"The Middle-Child Syndrome," "Family Dynamics in a Changing World"
Titles of articles or parts of books in the reference list: Use sentence-style capitalization.	The middle-child syndrome, Family dynamics in a changing world
Nouns used with numbers or letters in describing sequenced methods or examples	Day 4, Experiment 6, Table 1, Figure 3
Formal titles of tests	Scholastic Aptitude Test
Table and figure titles: Use headline-style capitalization.	*Grade Ranges of Remedial Students*
Column headers in tables: Use sentence-style capitalization.	Degree program, Years of experience, Kind of classroom
First word of a sentence that follows a colon	One challenge could not be met: The cost of the procedure was too great.
Running head (all capitals)	BEYOND BIRTH ORDER, TEST QUESTIONS

NOTE: Retain irregular capitalization patterns in trademarked product names: PowerPoint, iPad, WordPerfect, eBay.

SPECIAL CASES—NO CAPITALIZATION	EXAMPLES
General references to departments and courses	a number of departments of sociology, a speech pathology course
Generic or scientific names of drugs or ingredients	fluoxetine hydrochloride (*but* Prozac)
General titles of tests	an achievement test

Capitalization of Titles

APA follows two distinct patterns for the capitalization of titles: one within the text of a paper and one in the reference list and other supporting pages.

- **Parenthetical capitalization.** In the text of a paper, both in your prose and in parenthetical citations, use headline-style capitalization, no matter what kind of source you use. (See page 51.)
- **Reference-list (and other) capitalization.** In the reference list, only periodical titles use headline-style capitalization. The titles of articles and all other sources (such as books or films) use sentence-style capitalization. (See page 51.)
- **Capitalization of special in-text elements.** Headline-style capitalization is used for titles of tables and figures.

Article Title in the Text

In "Partners in Treatment: Relational Psychoanalysis and Harm Reduction Therapy," Rothschild (2010) described and analyzed two approaches to the treatment of at-risk patients, as well as advocated for efforts to integrate their techniques.

Article Title in a Reference-List Entry

Rothschild, D. (2010). Partners in treatment: Relational psychoanalysis and harm reduction therapy. *Journal of Clinical Psychology, 66*(2), 136–149. https://doi.org/10.1002/jcjp.20670

Book Title in the Text

In *The Mismeasure of Man*, Gould (1981) provided useful insights into the ethical and unethical uses to which intelligence tests can be put.

Book Title in a Reference-List Entry

Gould, S. J. (1981). *The mismeasure of man*. Norton.

NOTE: The running head of your written work appears in all capital letters.

Headline-Style Capitalization

GUIDING PRINCIPLES	EXAMPLES
Capitalize the first and last word; capitalize all other words except articles, *to* (as part of an infinitive phrase), and conjunctions or prepositions of three or fewer letters.	Edwards's *Post-Operative Stress: A Guide for the Family*, "Agent of Change: The Educational Legacy of Thomas Dewey"

Sentence-Style Capitalization

GUIDING PRINCIPLES	EXAMPLES
Capitalize the first word of a title or subtitle; otherwise, capitalize only proper nouns and proper adjectives.	Edwards's *Post-operative stress: A guide for the family*, "Agent of change: The educational legacy of Thomas Dewey"

Italics

APA requires the use of italics (slanted fonts, as in *this example*), rather than underlining.

USES OF ITALICS	EXAMPLES
Titles of full-length works: periodicals, books, films, CDs, webpages or subsites (but not websites), and so on	*Journal of Cognitive Psychology* (journal), *Wordplay and Language Learning* (book), *A Beautiful Mind* (film), *Back to Black* (CD), *Adolescent and School Health* (webpage) (but Centers for Disease Control and Prevention, a website)
Genus, species, or varieties	*Pan troglodytes verus* (common chimpanzee)
New terms (when introduced and defined; thereafter, presented without italics)	The term *Nisei*, meaning second-generation Japanese Americans
Words or letters that are linguistically identified as words or letters. (Alternately, they can be placed in quotation marks; see page 46.)	Different impressions are created by the words *small*, *diminutive*, *minute*, and *tiny*.

USES OF ITALICS	EXAMPLES
Words that could be misread	*More* specific detail (meaning additional detail that is specific)
Letters used as symbols or algebraic variables	$IQ = \dfrac{MA \text{ (mental age)}}{CA \text{ (chronological age)}} \times 100$
Titles of tables and figures	*Factors That Influence School Choice*
Volume numbers for periodicals (in reference-list entries)	American Journal of Nursing, *112*; Developmental Psychology, *48*
Anchors for scales	Satisfaction ratings ranged from 1 (*very satisfied*) to 8 (*very dissatisfied*).

Number Style

In APA style, numerals are used more frequently than words, whether in written texts or supporting materials; Arabic numerals are preferred in an APA-style text, rather than Roman numerals.

USES OF NUMERALS	EXAMPLES
Numbers of 10 and larger	14 respondents, 26 chapters, 11th article
Numbers smaller than 10 when compared with numbers larger than 10	the 4th chapter of 20; 2 of 30 research subjects; 13 sources, including 10 articles and 3 books
Numbers preceding units of measurement	6-in. mark, 300-mg capsule
Numbers used statistically or mathematically	7.5 of respondents, a ratio of 5:2, 9% of the sample, the 3rd percentile
Numbers that represent periods of time	6 years, 5 months, 1 week, 3 hours, 15 minutes, 7:15 p.m.
Numbers that represent dates	November 1, 2019; April 15, 2020
Numbers that represent ages	4-year-olds, students who are 8 years old

continued on next page

Punctuation and Mechanics

USES OF NUMERALS	EXAMPLES
Numbers for population size	1 million citizens
Numbers that refer to participants or subjects	7 participants, 4 rhesus monkeys
Numbers that refer to points or scores on a scale	a score of 6.5 on an 8-point scale
Numbers for exact sums of money	a DVD costing $24.25, a $35 fee
Numbers that indicate placement in a series	Exam 4, Figure 9
Numbers for parts of books	Chapter 2, page 6
Numbers in a list of four or more numbers	The sample was composed of work groups with 2, 4, 6, and 8 members.

USES OF WORDS FOR NUMBERS	EXAMPLES
Numbers smaller than 10 (see exceptions in the previous table)	two experimental models, three lists, a one-topic discussion
Zero and one (when confusion is likely)	zero-percent increase, one-unit design
Numbers that begin sentences	Sixteen authors contributed to the collection. Thirteen people attended.
Numbers that begin titles	"Twelve Common Errors in Research," *Seven-Point Scales: Values and Limitations*
Numbers that begin headings	*Five common income groups*
Numbers in common fractions	two thirds of teachers, a reduction of three fourths
Numbers in common names and phrases	the Seven Deadly Sins, the Ten Commandments, the Seven Wonders of the World

Cardinal and Ordinal Numbers

Cardinal numbers (one, two, three, and so on) indicate quantity; ordinal numbers (first, second, third, and so on) indicate order. The principles described in the preceding tables apply whether the numbers are cardinal or ordinal.

Commas in Numbers

In most writing contexts, commas are used in numbers of 1,000 or larger. Place commas between groups of three digits, moving from the right. However, in the following situations, commas are not used.

NUMBERS WITHOUT COMMAS	EXAMPLES
Page numbers	page 1287, pages 1002–1021, (p. 1349)
Degrees of temperature	2044°F
Serial numbers	033776901
Binary digits	01100100
Numbers to the right of decimal points	2.09986
Designations of acoustical frequency	1000 hz
Degrees of freedom	$F(31, 1000)$

Plurals of Numbers

Whether numbers are presented as numerals or words, form their plurals by adding only *s* or *es*: 1960s, threes, sixes, 25s. Do not use apostrophes to indicate plurality.

Numbered Seriation

To indicate series, sequences, or alternatives in a series of set-off sentences or paragraphs, use Arabic numerals, followed by periods (see page 38).

3b General Style

The way in which a manuscript is written affects the ways in which readers respond. A well-written paper communicates ideas efficiently and effectively, whereas a poorly written paper distracts readers from its central ideas. Therefore, take time to revise your writing to improve its presentation, paying special attention to elements that improve the effectiveness of communication.

Transitions

Transitions—words or phrases that signal relationships among elements of your writing—facilitate readers' progress through a paper. Use transitional words and phrases to create appropriate links within your work.

Transitional Words and Phrases

RELATIONSHIP	EXAMPLES
Addition	also, and, besides, equally, further, furthermore, in addition, moreover, next, too
Similarity	also, likewise, moreover, similarly
Difference	but, however, in contrast, nevertheless, on the contrary, on the other hand, yet
Examples	for example, for instance, in fact, specifically, to illustrate
Restatements	finally, in brief, in conclusion, in other words, in short, in summary, on the whole, that is, therefore, to sum up
Results	accordingly, as a result, consequently, for this reason, so, therefore, thereupon, thus
Chronology	after, afterward, before, during, earlier, finally, first, immediately, in the meantime, later, meanwhile, next, second, simultaneously, soon, still, then, third, when, while
Location	above, below, beyond, farther, here, nearby, opposite, there, to the left, to the right, under

Verb Tense

Verbs are primary communicators in sentences, signaling action (*organized, summarized, presented*) or indicating a state of being (*seemed, was*). Well-chosen, specific verbs make writing direct and forceful. Moreover, tenses of verbs indicate chronology, clarifying the time relationships that you want to express.

In APA style, verbs are used in specific ways to signal ideas clearly.

USES OF VERBS	EXAMPLES
Active voice (to clarify who is doing what)	Respondents completed the questionnaire in 15 minutes. (*Not:* The questionnaire was completed in 15 minutes by the respondents.)
Passive voice (to clarify who or what received the action, not the person or people responsible)	Traditional IQ tests were administered as part of the admissions process. (The use of the tests is emphasized, not the givers of the tests.)
Past tense (to place an action in the past or to describe previous research)	Bradshaw and Hines (2017) summarized their results in one incisive paragraph.
Present perfect tense (to describe an action that began in the past and continues to the present or to describe a concept with continued application)	In the years since, researchers have incorporated Piaget's methods in a variety of studies of children.
Subjunctive mood (to describe a conditional situation or one contrary to fact)	If the sampling were larger, the results might be different.

Agreement

Agreement is the matching of words or word forms according to number (singular and plural) and gender (masculine, feminine, or neuter). Verbs take singular or plural forms depending on whether their subjects are singular or plural.

Subject–Verb Agreement

SPECIAL CIRCUMSTANCES	EXAMPLES
Foreign words—*datum* (singular) versus *data* (plural), *phenomenon* (singular) versus *phenomena* (plural), and others: Choose the correct form.	The data suggest that our preconceptions were ill founded. (plural subject/plural verb) The phenomenon is unlikely to occur again. (singular subject/singular verb)

continued on next page

General Style

SPECIAL CIRCUMSTANCES	EXAMPLES
Collective (or group) nouns: Consider whether members of the group act in unison (singular) or individually (plural).	The couple initiates the counseling sessions. (singular meaning to stress shared action) The couple meet separately with the counselor. (plural meaning to stress separate actions)
Singular and plural subjects joined by *or* or *nor*: Match the verb to the nearer subject.	Neither the parents nor the therapist finds their meetings helpful. Or: Neither the therapist nor the parents find their meetings helpful.

Pronoun–Antecedent Agreement

Pronouns must match their antecedents (the words to which they refer) in both number and gender.

COMMON CIRCUMSTANCES	EXAMPLES
Agreement in number: Match the pronoun to its antecedent. (*Also see* "Biased Language," pages 60–62.)	A participant secures his or her stipend from the controller's office. (singular) Participants secure their stipends from the controller's office. (plural)
Agreement in gender: Match the pronoun to the antecedent. (*Also see* "Biased Language.")	Devon was the first student to complete his exam. (masculine) The lab rat (subject 3) stopped eating its food during the experiment. (neuter)
Who and *whom*: Use *who* in a subject position; use *whom* in an object position.	Who is responsible for compiling the data? (subject: *He* is; *she* is; *they* are.) To whom should we address our inquiries? (object: Address inquiries to *him*; address inquiries to *her*; address inquiries to *them*.)

Parallelism

Parallelism is the use of equivalent forms when words are used together: nouns, verbs of the same tense or form, and so on.

PARALLELS	EXAMPLES
Elements in a series: Use matching forms.	Even young children are expected to add, to subtract, and to multiply. (parallel verb forms) Reading, writing, speaking, listening, and thinking compose the language arts. (parallel gerund/noun forms)
Correlative conjunctions (*both/and, either/or, neither/nor, not only/but also*): Use matching forms of the words, phrases, and clauses that are linked.	The youngest child in a large family is either the most independent or the least independent of the siblings. (parallel phrases) We found not only that the experiment was too costly but also that it was too time consuming. (parallel clauses)

3c Word Choice

Word choice makes meaning clear to readers. Specific word choices affect the tone of writing—implying your perception of yourself, your readers, your subject, and your purpose in writing. Consequently, choose words carefully to communicate ideas effectively.

Noun Clusters

Noun clusters are created when nouns, often in multiples, are used to modify yet another noun. Although the modification patterns may be grammatically correct (nouns *can* function as modifiers), they often create dense clusters of meaning that have to be sorted through carefully.

For example, the phrase *first-year student success ensurance initiative* is overly long, does not read smoothly, and has to be deconstructed. To improve readability, untangle the nouns and place them in easily readable phrases: *an initiative to ensure the success of first-year students*. The reconstructed phrase is easier to interpret than the original and, therefore, communicates the idea more efficiently than does the original.

Jargon

Jargon is the specialized language of a professional group. In some instances, a specific technical term communicates an idea more efficiently than an explanation in everyday language. For instance, the phrase *correlational analyses* explains in two generally understood words a process by which data are both systematically linked and logically compared. However, in many instances, common language that is well selected communicates ideas in a more straightforward and less pretentious way than jargon does. For example, in many instances, the phrase *classroom teacher* communicates an idea with greater clarity and less distraction than the more affected phrase *teacher/practitioner*, which is a stilted way of expressing an idea that is implicit in the word *teacher*.

In your writing, choose words with care. Use technical jargon only when it communicates ideas clearly and efficiently—that is, when it is precise and helpful. Never use jargon to impress, because an over-reliance on technical terms (especially those that do not communicate ideas precisely and quickly) frustrates readers and clutters prose.

Colloquialisms

In academic writing, avoid colloquialisms—expressions that are better suited for conversation and other forms of informal communication. Words and phrases such as *write-up* (instead of *report*), *only a few* (rather than 7%), or *get-together* (in place of *meeting* or *colloquium*) not only lack the specificity of more technical, formal language but also suggest a lack of precision that may make readers question the care with which you have described your research. For these reasons, use precise, professional language in your writing.

Specificity

Choose specific words to create clear meaning; do not assume that readers will infer meaning from vague language. For example, rather than writing that a survey contained *numerous questions*, be specific and indicate that it contained *45 questions*. Instead of noting that a study was based on the responses of *many Midwestern students*, describe the research group more precisely: *2,000 first-year college students in Missouri and Iowa*. Even this description could be made more specific by noting the percentage of male/female respondents, the kinds of schools (liberal arts colleges, small state universities, large state universities, and so on), and the locations of the schools (urban, rural, and so on).

The credibility of research depends on using language that communicates clearly. Consequently, choose words that are as specific as possible.

Biased Language

Whether employed consciously or unconsciously, the use of biased language conveys a writer's insensitivity, ignorance, or, in some instances, prejudice—any of which disrupts communication. Writing that incorporates biased language reflects badly on the writer, alienates thoughtful readers, and consequently interferes with effective communication.

As a writer, you should make a conscious effort to use accurate, equitable language. Recognizing that your potential readers represent a broad spectrum of society, choose words with care and avoid stereotypes.

Racial and Ethnic Bias

Language that is racially and ethnically biased often relies on dated words related to racial or ethnic groups. In other instances, racially and ethnically biased word choices ignore the distinct groups that exist within larger classifications, thereby perpetuating broad stereotypes. Consequently, it is preferable to refer to racial or ethnic groups as specifically as possible.

Preferred Racial or Ethnic Terms

QUESTIONABLE	PREFERRED TERMS FOR AMERICAN CITIZENS	PREFERRED TERMS FOR NON-AMERICAN CITIZENS
Arab	Arab American; *or* Saudi American, Iraqi American, and so on	Saudi, Iraqi, Afghan, and so on
Hispanic	Latino/Latina, Chicano/Chicana; *or* Cuban American and so on	Mexican, Cuban, Costa Rican, and so on
Indian	Native American; *or* Cherokee, Ogallal Sioux, Seminole, and so on	Mesoamerican, Inuit, and so on

continued on next page

QUESTIONABLE	PREFERRED TERMS FOR AMERICAN CITIZENS	PREFERRED TERMS FOR NON-AMERICAN CITIZENS
Black	African American; *or* Kenyan American and so on	African; *or* Ugandan, Kenyan, and so on
White	European American; *or* Italian American, French American, Irish American, and so on	Caucasian, European; *or* German, French, Hungarian, Russian, and so on
Oriental	Asian American; *or* Japanese American, Korean American, Chinese American, and so on	Asian; *or* Korean, Japanese, Vietnamese, and so on

Gender Bias

Language based on stereotypical gender roles—also called sexist language—implies through choices of nouns, pronouns, and adjectives that people fall into preassigned roles. Because gender-biased language fails to reflect the diversity of contemporary society, it is inaccurate. Replace nouns that imply gender exclusivity—for example, *chairman* or *spokesman*—with gender-neutral alternatives—for example, *chairperson* or *spokesperson*.

Avoid using gender-specific pronouns when their antecedents are not gender specific. The most common concern is the generic use of a masculine pronoun (*he, him, his, himself*), as in this sentence: "A psychiatrist is bound by professional oath to keep his patients' records confidential." Although this usage was once acceptable, today's writers and readers expect pronoun use to be inclusive, not exclusionary. Consider these alternative solutions:

- **Use plural forms.** Rather than use a singular noun to describe a general or universal situation, use a plural noun and plural pronoun instead: "Psychiatrists are bound by professional oath to keep their patients' records confidential." This pattern stresses that the circumstances apply to many people in many contexts, rather than implying that the action is unique or individual.

- **Use the "singular *they*."** APA style no longer sanctions the use of alternative pronoun forms ("he or she"); instead, APA recommends the use of the "singular *they*": "A psychiatrist

is bound by professional oath to keep their patients' records confidential." This pattern makes no assumptions about the psychiatrist's gender and reduces the possibly of bias.
- **Omit pronouns.** When no confusion is likely, you can omit the pronoun: "A psychiatrist is bound by professional oath to keep patients' records confidential." This pattern stresses the action; further, it clarifies that patients and their records do not "belong" to a psychiatrist.

Avoid using gender-related adjectives when other modifiers create similar meaning without bias or when gender is not an issue. "The male nurse was both competent and friendly, reassuring the patient and family members" is better presented this way: "The nurse was both competent and friendly, reassuring the patient and family members."

Other Forms of Bias

Be sensitive to the ways in which your language characterizes people by age, class, religion, region, physical and mental ability, or sexual orientation. Do your word choices create stereotypical impressions that disrupt your discussions? Do they convey unintended but negative feelings? Will they offend potential readers and therefore distract them from your ideas? Examine your writing carefully for instances of these kinds of bias and explore alternative ways to convey your meaning.

Biased Language in a Historical Context

Historical texts often contain language that violates today's standards of usage. However, if you quote from such a text, you should retain the original language. The date in the parenthetical reference will allow readers to place the language in the correct historical context. If the language is particularly troublesome, you may insert an asterisk (*) following the first use of the word or phrase and provide commentary in a footnote.

4 Preparing the Reference List and Parenthetical Citations

Chapter Objectives:

- Learn what information is required for reference-list entries.
- Learn how to format reference-list entries.
- Learn how to prepare parenthetical citations.
- Learn how to incorporate quotations in the text.

The reference list provides comprehensive information on each of the sources used in a paper. By listing the author (or authors) of each source—along with publication dates, full titles, and information about publishers (producers, distributors, or websites)—writers ensure that readers can locate sources for further study.

Sources that appear in the reference list must be cited in the paper using parallel information. For example, if a reference-list entry includes two authors, then the parenthetical citation must also include both authors' names (see "Parenthetical Citations" later in this chapter). For this reason, writers should prepare reference-list entries for sources before writing the paper.

This chapter includes detailed discussions of the information required for a reference list, as well as its formatting requirements; Chapters 5 through 8 provide explanations and examples of the most commonly used sources for APA papers. In addition, this book provides information on some sources that are not traditionally used in APA journal articles (the writing done by professionals) but that are potentially useful for students' writing; the principles of APA documentation style have been applied in preparing these sample entries.

4a The Reference List—An Overview

A reference list is an alphabetically arranged listing of sources used in a paper. It starts on a new page immediately after the last text page of the paper, continues the page numbering, and is also double-spaced. It is introduced by the word *References* (centered, in boldface type, but not italicized); if the reference list continues on subsequent pages, no additional heading is required for those pages. Entries in the reference list follow the formats described in this chapter. (See pages 123 and 134 for the reference lists of the sample papers.)

4b Information for APA Entries

Entries for the reference list vary because of the different information they include. All, however, must follow an established order for presenting information.

1. **Authors (and editors).** Take names from the first page of an article or from the title page of a book (without titles or degree designations such as *Dr., Professor*, or *RN*). Search online sources carefully because authors' names are not always placed in the most logical locations. Authors' or editors' names are listed in the order in which they appear (not alphabetical order), and initials are used instead of first or middle names. *All* authors' names are inverted (last name first), not just the name of the first author. In some circumstances, groups, corporations, institutions, or organizations publish works under their collective names, rather than those of individual authors; in such cases, the names are spelled out completely. Up to twenty authors can be listed; however, if a work has twenty-one or more authors, list the names of the first nineteen authors, followed by ellipsis points (three spaced periods), and the name of the last author. *Note:* When a source has no author, the entry begins with the title, followed by the date.

2. **Publication dates.** For articles in scholarly journals and books, include the publication year in parentheses. For sources that use specific dates—such as popular magazines, newspapers, television broadcasts, or websites—include the year and the month or the year, month, and day in parentheses.

3. **Titles.** List titles completely, taking information from the first page of an article or from the title page of a book. Include both titles and subtitles, no matter how long they are.

4. **Additional information.** Include any of the following information in the order presented here if it is listed on the first page of the article, essay, chapter or other subsection, or the title page of the book:
   - Translator
   - Edition number
   - Volume number
   - Issue number
   - Inclusive pages

5. **Facts of publication.** For periodicals, take the volume number, issue number, and date from the first few pages in journals and magazines, often in combination with the table of contents, or from the masthead (a listing of

information at the top of the first page of newspapers). Take the publisher's name from the title page; you may use the complete form of the publisher's name or an abbreviated form, depending on your instructor's preference (see the box on page 68 for explanations of how to shorten publishers' names and Chapters 5 through 8 for samples within entries). Use the most recent date from the copyright page (which immediately follows the title page).

6. **Retrieval information.** For electronic sources, provide digital object identifiers (DOIs) or universal resource locators (URLs) as freestanding elements; retrieval statements are unnecessary.

DECODING DELINQUENCY

PSYCHOLOGICAL AND SOCIAL FACTORS THAT INFLUENCE YOUTH BEHAVIOR

Revised Edition

Marcus J. Dickerson
Kathryn P. Andrews

C. C. Hanford & Sons
Boston   Chicago   Dallas   London

Sample title page

- Authors (last names and initials; in the order on the title page)
- Date (the most recent one); see the sample copyright page on page 66.
- Title (including the subtitle)
- Edition (in abbreviated form)
- Publisher (in shortened form)

Dickerson, M. J., & Andrews, K. P. (2019). Decoding delinquency: Psychological and social factors that influence youth behavior (Rev. ed.). Hanford.

C. C. HANFORD & SONS

Boston   Chicago   Dallas   London

C. C. Hanford & Sons
214 Channel Street, Boston, MA 02211, USA

Published in the United States by C. C. Hanford & Sons, Boston

www.cchanford.com
Information on this title: www.cchanford.com/94284301

© 2009, 2019 C. C. Hanford & Sons

ALL RIGHTS RESERVED. No part of this work covered by the copyright herein may be reproduced, transmitted, stored, or used in any form or by any means graphic, electronic, or mechanical, including but not limited to photocopying, recording, scanning, digitizing, taping, Web distribution, information networks, or information storage and retrieval systems, except as permitted under Section 107 or 108 of the 1976 United States Copyright Act, without the prior permission of the publisher.

First printed 2009
Reprinted 2010 (twice)

Printed in the United States

ISBN-13: 121-0-443-91263-6
ISBN-10: 0-443-91263-6

C. C. Hanford & Sons has no responsibility for the persistence or accuracy of URLs for external or third-party internet websites referred to in this book, and does not guarantee that any content on such websites is, or will remain, accurate or appropriate.

Sample copyright page

4c Format for APA Entries

To ensure easy reading, entries for the reference list must follow this format.

- **Indentation patterns.** Begin the first line of each entry at the left margin; indent subsequent lines five to seven spaces (½ inch), using the "Indent" feature.

Format for APA Entries

- **Authors' names.** Because entries must be arranged in alphabetical order, invert all authors' names (Haley, R.) and use an ampersand (&), not the word *and*, to join the names of multiple authors (Haley, R., & Taylor, J.).
- **Authorless sources.** When no author is identified, list the source by title. Alphabetize a reference-list entry by using the primary words of the title (excluding *a*, *an*, or *the*). When an authorless book has an editor, you can, as an alternative, begin the entry with the editor's last name and first and middle initials (with the abbreviation *Ed.* in parentheses but not italicized), followed by a period.
- **Article titles.** Include full titles, using sentence-style capitalization (see pages 50–51 for an explanation of capitalization patterns). Article titles are not enclosed in quotation marks in a reference-list entry, although they are placed in quotation marks and use headline-style capitalization (see page 51) in parenthetical citations and in the paper.
- **Periodical titles.** Present the titles of periodicals in headline style (see page 51). Follow the title with a comma and the volume number. Italicize the title *and* the volume number, including the separating comma and the comma that follows the volume number.
- **Issue numbers.** Place the issue number in parentheses after the volume number; no space separates the volume number from the issue number, and the parentheses and issue number are *not* italicized. Both volume and issue numbers are presented as Arabic, not Roman, numerals.
- **Titles of books.** Present the titles of books with sentence-style capitalization. The title is italicized. (However, headline-style capitalization is used in the paper.)
- **Publishers' names.** You may use publishers' names in full form or shorten the names of commercial publishers to brief but clear forms, using only the main elements of their names (Cengage, not Cengage Learning) and dropping descriptive titles (Publishers, Company, Incorporated). However, use the complete names of organizations and corporations that serve as publishers and university presses, retaining the words *Books* and *Press* whenever they are part of a publisher's name. If a work has co-publishers, include both publishers' names, separated by a semicolon (Harvard; Belknap Press). (See the "Shortened Forms" box for guidelines and examples.)
- **Punctuation within entries.** Separate major sections of entries (author, date, title, and publication information) with periods, including elements enclosed in parentheses or brackets; the period used with the abbreviation of an author's

first or middle name substitutes for this period. When an entry ends with a DOI or URL, no period is required to close the entry.

Shortened Forms of Publishers' Names

Use the full names of associations and corporations that serve as publishers.	American Psychological Association, National Council of Teachers of English (These publishers' names appear in their full forms.)
Use the full names of university presses.	Harvard University Press, University of Illinois Press (These publishers' names appear in their full forms.)
Use full names for government publishers.	U.S. Government Printing Office (This name appears in its full form.)
Drop given names or initials.	Harry N. Abrams is shortened to Abrams.
Use the first of multiple names.	Farrar, Straus, and Giroux is shortened to Farrar.
Drop corporation designations: *Publishers, Company, Incorporated,* and so on.	Doubleday and Co., Inc. is shortened to Doubleday.
Retain the words *Books* and *Press*.	Bantam Books, American Psychiatric Press (These publishers' names appear in their full forms.)

- **Spacing within entries.** One space separates elements in APA entries. However, the issue number (in parentheses) follows the volume number without a space.
- **Abbreviations.** Use abbreviations for standard parts of periodicals, books, and other print materials. (See the "Acceptable Abbreviations" box for examples.)
- **Page numbers.** When citing articles in periodicals or chapters or other portions of complete works, list numbers completely (pp. 176–179, not pp. 176–9 or pp. 176–79), separated by a

hyphen or an en dash. Journals and magazines list page numbers without page abbreviations; however, page references for newspapers, books, and other print materials use the abbreviations *p.* (for page) and *pp.* (for pages), not italicized. No commas are used to separate digits of numbers one thousand or larger when citing pages (pp. 1295–1298). When articles appear on non-consecutive pages, list all pages, separated by commas (pp. 34–35, 38, 54–55, 57, 59).

- **Line spacing.** The entire reference list is double-spaced.

Acceptable Abbreviations

edition	ed.
Editor (Editors)	Ed. (Eds.)
no date	n.d.
no publisher	n.p.
Number	No.
page (pages)	p. (pp.)
paragraph (paragraphs)	para. (paras.)
Part	Pt.
Revised edition	Rev. ed.
Second edition, fifth edition	2nd ed., 5th ed. (superscript is not used)
Supplement	Suppl.
Technical report	Tech. Rep.
Translator	Trans.
Volume (Volumes)	Vol. (Vols.)

4d Alphabetizing the Reference List

The reference list must be in alphabetical order, which seems simple enough. Reality often proves more complicated, however, so use the guidelines in the "Alphabetizing" box.

Alphabetizing the Reference List

CIRCUMSTANCES	*RULE AND SAMPLE*
Letter-by-letter style	Alphabetize one letter at a time: *Baker, R. L.* precedes *Baker, W. S.; Our American Heritage* comes before *Our American Legacy*.
"Nothing precedes something"	The space that follows a name supersedes the letters that follow: *Wood, T. S.,* precedes *Woodman, K. F.*
Prefixes	Prefixes are alphabetized as they appear, not as if they appeared in full form: *MacDonald, J. B.,* precedes *McDonald, B. V.*
Names with prepositions	Names that incorporate prepositions are alphabetized as if they were spelled closed: *De Forest, A. M.,* precedes *Denton, R. L.* (Consult a dictionary regarding patterns for names in different languages.)
Multiple works by the same author	Arrange selections in chronological order: *Sparks, C. G.* (2017) precedes *Sparks, C. G.* (2019)
Single-author and multiple-author works	Single-author works precede multiple-author works: *Kelly, M. J.,* precedes *Kelly, M. J., & Davidson, P. G.*
Groups, institutions, or organizations as authors	Alphabetize group, institutional, or organizational authors by major words in their completely spelled-out names (omitting *a*, *an*, or *the*): *American Psychological Association* precedes *Anderson, V. W.*
Authorless works	Authorless works are alphabetized by the first significant words in their titles (omitting *a*, *an*, or *the*): *The price of poverty* precedes *Stewart, R. P.*
Numerals in titles	Numerals in titles are alphabetized as if they were spelled out: "The 10 common errors of research" precedes *Twelve angry men*.

4e Parenthetical Citations

APA documentation has two areas of emphasis: (a) the authors of source materials and (b) the year in which sources were published or presented. This pattern is commonly referred to as the author–date style.

When incorporating information from a source, provide a parenthetical citation that includes, at minimum, the author's last name and the year of publication or presentation. The complexity of some sources may require the inclusion of additional information.

Patterns for Parenthetical Citations

A parenthetical citation corresponds to an entry in the reference list at the end of the paper. The information in an entry for the reference list determines what information appears in a parenthetical citation in the text. For example, if a reference-list entry for a source begins with the author's name, then the author's name appears in the parenthetical citation. If a reference-list citation for a source begins with the title, however, then the title (or a shortened version of it) appears in the parenthetical citation. If these correlations are clear and consistent, readers can turn from the paper's parenthetical citation to the reference list and easily locate the full entry for the source.

Basic Forms of Parenthetical Citations

To avoid disrupting the text, parenthetical citations identify only the last name of the author (or authors) or a brief version of the title under which the source appears in the reference list, followed by the year of publication (even when reference-list entries require the month or month and day). For the sake of clarity and smoothness, you may incorporate some of the necessary information in your sentences. After the author and date have been introduced, the date may be omitted in subsequent references within the same paragraph.

> Educational bodies—accrediting agencies, boards of education, and school boards—must acknowledge that assessment of teaching performance may focus on different issues: "Evaluating whether teachers promote student learning is one thing, while evaluating whether they raise student test scores is another" (Papay, 2012, pp. 131–132). Unless they do so, assessment will be ineffective, and the results will be potentially damaging.

OR

> Educational bodies—accrediting agencies, boards of education, and school boards—must acknowledge that assessment of teaching

performance may focus on different issues. Papay (2012) observed that "evaluating whether teachers promote student learning is one thing, while evaluating whether they raise student test scores is another" (pp. 131–132). Unless this difference is noted, assessment will be ineffective, and the results will be potentially damaging.

Reference-list entry

Papay, J. N. (2012). Refocusing the debate: Assessing the purposes and tools of teacher evaluation. *Harvard Educational Review, 82*(1), 123–141. https://doi.org/10.19963/haer.82.1.v40p0833345w6384

Shortened Forms of Titles

- **Use initial words of the title.** Because readers will use the short title to find the full title in the reference list, use words at the beginning. "When Teachers Don't Make the Grade" can logically be shortened to "When Teachers."
- **Omit articles.** *A, an,* and *the* should be dropped from the shortened title. *A Long Day's Journey into Night* can be shortened to *Long Day's Journey.*
- **Omit subtitles.** Omit the clarifying information in the second part of a two-part title. "Paycare: The High Cost of Insurance-based Medicine" can be shortened to "Paycare."
- **Omit prepositional phrases.** Omit prepositional phrases at the ends of titles. *The Price of Poverty* can be shortened to *Price.*
- **Make the short title brief but readable.** Remember that the short title will be part of your text and should, consequently, read well. *The Chicago Manual of Style* shortens to *Chicago Manual; Chicago* alone might be confusing or unclear.
- **Retain punctuation patterns.** Follow the punctuation patterns required in the text: Titles of articles, chapters, poems, and other brief works are placed in quotation marks; titles of journals, books, films, and other long works are italicized. Punctuate the shortened forms of titles as you would the complete forms. *APA Dictionary of Psychology* can be shortened to *APA Dictionary*, but it remains in italics.

In special cases, the rule of using only the author's last name and the date is superseded.

Patterns for Parenthetical Citations

CIRCUMSTANCES	RULE AND SAMPLE
Two authors with the same last name	Include initials with the last name: (Barratt, J. D., 2018), distinct from (Barratt, L. K., 2016).
Multiple works by the same author (same year)	Use letters to distinguish the sources: (Morrison, 2019a), distinct from (Morrison, 2019b). The letters indicate the alphabetical order of the titles.
Multiple works by the same author (same note)	To cite several works by the same author (all included in the reference list), include the author's name and all dates in chronological order, separated by commas: (Vidich, 2016, 2018, 2019).
Three or more authors	Include the first author's last name and the abbreviation *et al.,* (which means "and others" and is not italicized), followed by the publication date: (Greeley et al., 2018).
Three or more authors (when some additional authors are the same)	Include as many names as necessary to avoid confusion: (Austen, Bentley, Davidson, Perkins, et al., 2018) is distinguished from (Austen, Bentley, Davidson, Shafer, et al., 2017).
Two or more works by different authors (same note)	To cite several works by different authors in the same note, list each author (in alphabetical order) and date, separated by semicolons: (Bennet, 2016; Greene, 2019; Swift, 2017).
Organization as author	In the first note, present the organization's name in full, with an abbreviation in brackets: (American Association of Community Psychiatrists [AACP], 2019). Use the abbreviation in subsequent citations: (AACP, 2019).

continued on next page

CIRCUMSTANCES	RULE AND SAMPLE
No author	Include a shortened version of the title, appropriately capitalized and punctuated, and the year: ("Optimum Performance," 2020); (*Common Ground*, 2017). If *Anonymous* is the *explicit* attribution of a work, it is used in the author position, but not italicized: (Anonymous, 2019).
Multiple publication dates	Include both dates, separated by a slash: (Jagger & Richards, 1994/2001).
Reference works	List by author if applicable (Sternberg, 2020) or by a shortened form of the title ("Artificial Intelligence," 2018).
Parts of sources	When citing only a portion of a source—for example, a page to identify a quotation or a chapter in a general reference—include the author or title as appropriate, the date, and clarifying information: (Thomas, 2018, p. 451); (Spindrell, 2019, Chapters 2–3).
Personal communication	Cite email, correspondence, memos, interviews, and so on by listing the person's name, the clarifying phrase *personal communication* (not italicized), and the specific date (L. R. Bates, personal communication, March 7, 2019).

NOTE: Although cited in the text, personal communications do not have entries in the reference list. Initials are also used with the person's last name.

4f Quotations

When an author's manner of expression is unique or when ideas or language are difficult to paraphrase or summarize, quote the passage in your text. To avoid plagiarism, reproduce quoted material word for word (including exact spelling and punctuation), separate the material from your text, and prepare an accurate citation.

The pattern for incorporating a quotation varies depending on its length. Parenthetical citations for quotations also include specific page references.

Brief Quotations (Fewer Than 40 Words)

A quotation of fewer than 40 words appears within a normal paragraph, with the author's words enclosed in quotation marks. The parenthetical citation follows the closing quotation mark, whether it is in the middle or at the end of a sentence; if the quotation ends the sentence, the sentence's period follows the closing parenthesis. The citation includes the author's name and the publication date (unless these have been previously mentioned in the text), as well as a specific page reference, introduced with the abbreviation *p.* or *pp.* (not italicized). For example:

> The law is inextricably linked to culture and, at times, popular culture. Reacting to controversial films about teenagers in the 1950s, "both civil rights activists and segregationists harnessed popular outrage and fear over delinquent youth" (Walker, 2010, p. 1913). The result was a cultural collision about race, class, and ethnicity.

Reference-list entry

Walker, A. (2010). Blackboard jungle: Delinquency, desegregation, and the cultural politics of Brown. *Columbia Law Review, 110*(7), 1911–1953. https://doi.org/10.2307/27896313

Long Quotations (40 or More Words)

A quotation of 40 or more words is set off from a normal paragraph in an indented block paragraph. After an introductory statement, start the quotation on a new line, indented five to seven spaces or ½ inch (use the "Indent" feature to maintain the indentation throughout the quotation). Quotation marks do not appear at the opening and closing of a block quotation. Like the surrounding text, the quotation is double-spaced. Note that the period precedes the parenthetical citation with a block quotation. For example:

> Expressing current uncertainty about the causes of allergy patterns, Prescott and Allen (2011) observed:
> > Allergic disease has been linked to the modern lifestyle including changing dietary patterns, changing intestinal commensal bacteria and vehicular pollution. It is not yet known whether the rise in food allergy is a harbinger of earlier and more severe effects of these pervasive environmental changes or whether additional or unrelated lifestyle factors are implicated. (p. 155)

In modern societies, which prize both certainty and attributable blame, this kind of inconclusiveness is disturbing.

Reference-list entry

Prescott, S., & Allen, K. J. (2011). Food allergy: Riding the second wave of the allergy epidemic. *Pediatric Allergy and Immunology, 22*(2), 155–160. https://doi.org/10.1111/j.1399-3038.2011.01145.x

---

Concerns About Quotations

Although quotations can enhance a paper by presenting the ideas of other writers in their own words, the overuse of quotations can become distracting. Some instructors even advise against using quotations in papers—suggesting, instead, that the ideas should be summarized or paraphrased. Therefore, assess the value of quotations by asking the following questions and use quotations selectively.

- **Style.** Is the style so distinctive that you cannot say the same thing as well or as clearly in your own words?
- **Vocabulary.** Is the vocabulary technical and therefore difficult to translate into your own words?
- **Reputation.** Is the author so well known or so important that the quotation can lend authority to your paper?
- **Points of contention.** Does the author's material raise doubts or questions or make points with which you disagree? Rather than potentially misrepresenting a view with which you disagree, quote the source.

If you answer yes to any of these questions, then using the quotation is appropriate. If not, summarize or paraphrase the material instead.

Punctuation With Quotations

Single Quotation Marks

To indicate an author's use of quotation marks within a brief quotation (which is set off by double quotation marks), change the source's punctuation to single quotation marks, as in this example:

In an effort to contextualize and to clarify the current debate about gun laws, Brandl and Stroshine (2010) stated that "the distinction between the 'legal' gun market and the 'illegal' gun market is a fuzzy one, at best. The distinction relates most directly to how the gun was acquired, the characteristics of the person who acquired the gun, and how the gun has been used" (p. 287). In other words, to advance the debate logically, the full context must be established.

Reference-list entry

Brandl, S. G., & Stroshine, M. S. (2010). The relationship between gun and gun buyer characteristics and firearm time-to-crime. *Criminal Justice Policy Review, 22*(3), 285–300. https://doi.org/10.1177/0887403410373510

Because long block quotations do not begin and end with quotation marks, the source's quotation marks remain double, as in this example:

> Skolnick (2010) noted that police behavior, from one perspective, developed because of work experiences, but also observed:
>> An alternative explanation for police behavior suggested that the characteristics, values, and opinions [officers bring] with them to [the] job were better predictors of behavior. Police work attracted certain types of people whose behavior was more a product of their general personality, not any "working personality" formed on the job. (p. 10)

Until additional studies are completed, this "nature versus nurture" debate will continue.

Reference-list entry

Skolnick, J. (2010). Police personality: Are police officers different from the rest of us? In A. B. Thistlethwaite & J. D. Wooldredge (Eds.), *Forty studies that changed criminal justice: Explorations into the history of criminal justice research* (pp. 6–13). Pearson; Prentice Hall.

Brackets

Use brackets to indicate that you have either added words for clarity or introduced a substitution within a quotation. Most often, the words you add will be specific nouns to substitute for pronouns that are vague outside the context of the original work. However, you may substitute a different tense of the same verb (for example, *used* for *use*). *NOTE:* A change in the capitalization at the beginning of a sentence, as well as a change in end punctuation to fit your syntax, does not require the use of brackets.

In assessing issues of America's increasing obesity, Oliver (2006) observed that the "BMI [Body-Mass Index] remains the basis for much of our official health policy today, both in the way we think of obesity and how we measure it" (p. 20). However, weight, by itself, is not the only predictor of health.

The complete form of the abbreviation provides clarity for readers.

Reference-list entry

Oliver, J. E. (2006). *Fat politics: The real story behind America's obesity epidemic.* Oxford University Press.

NOTE: Do not change dated language or material to make it more acceptable by today's standards; rather, let the material stand on its own and provide your own separate commentary. (See page 62.)

Ellipsis Points

Use ellipsis points—three spaced periods—to indicate where words have been omitted within a quotation. Ellipsis points are unnecessary at the beginning or end of a quotation, unless a quotation begins or ends in the middle of a sentence. To indicate an omission between sentences, retain the preceding sentence's punctuation (producing four spaced periods).

Epstein (2012) explained the learning challenge of older adults in this way:
> As we age, the degradation of sensory and working memory systems makes it increasingly difficult for us to transfer information into long-term storage. That's why, if you are over 50, you are more likely to remember the lyrics to a Beatles song than to any song you have heard in the past 20 years. . . . Our ability to learn new things is extraordinary when we are young and peaks in our teens. We can learn after that, but it becomes increasingly difficult. (pp. 50, 76)

This, in part, accounts for the difficulties that the older adults have in learning to use new technologies and dealing with new processes.

[Omission: "To put this another way . . . "]

Reference-list entry

Epstein, R. (2012, October). Brutal truths: About the aging brain. *Discover, 33*(8), 48–50, 76.

5 Citing Periodicals

Chapter Objectives:

- Learn to prepare reference-list entries for periodicals.
- Learn to prepare corresponding parenthetical citations.
- Learn to distinguish between primary and secondary sources.

Reference-List Entries for Periodicals

5a An Article in a Journal (80)
5b An Abstract (80)
5c An Article in a Monthly Magazine (81)
5d An Article in a Weekly Magazine (81)
5e An Article in a Newspaper (81)
5f An Article in a Newsletter (82)
5g An Editorial (82)
5h A Letter to the Editor (83)
5i A Review (83)
5j A Secondary Source (84)

Most often affiliated with professional organizations, journals are scholarly publications whose articles are subjected to careful review. Often called refereed journals, they are the mainstay of much research because they present ideas and information developed by scholars and specialists—and reviewed by scholars—for an audience of scholars. Magazines, in contrast, are commercial publications that present ideas and information for general readers who are nonspecialists; they provide nontechnical discussions and general reactions to issues. (For additional discussion, see pages 10–11.) Newspapers, published daily or weekly, provide nearly instantaneous reactions to issues in primary stories and more reflective discussions in editorials and feature articles. These periodicals provide reports on research and discussions of contemporary ideas and issues of importance to writers of researched papers.

To cite periodicals in a reference list, follow the guidelines given in this chapter.

5a   An Article in a Journal

To create a reference-list entry for an article in a journal, start with the author's name, followed by the year of publication in parentheses, followed by a period. Then include the title of the article with sentence-style capitalization (without quotation marks). Next, include the title of the journal (with headline-style capitalization), a comma, and the volume number (all italicized). Without a separating space, put the issue number in parentheses, followed by a comma; the parentheses, issue number, and the comma are not italicized. Finish the primary part of the entry by listing the inclusive page numbers, without a page abbreviation. If an article has a DOI or a URL link, include it at the end of the entry; no introductory phrase is necessary, and no period is used at the end of the entry. (See page 104 for a more detailed discussion of DOIs and URLs.)

Harrison, R. L., & Westwood, M. J. (2009). Preventing vicarious traumatization of mental health therapists: Identifying protective practices. *Psychotherapy Theory, Research, Practice, Training, 46*(2), 203–219. https://doi.org/10.1037/a0016081

   Parenthetical citation (Harrison & Westwood, 2009)

Kinports, K. (2011). The Supreme Court's love-hate relationship with Miranda. *Journal of Criminal Law and Criminology, 101*(2), 375–440. https://doi.org/0091-4169/11/1002-375

   Parenthetical citation (Kinports, 2011)

5b   An Abstract

Although writers most often refer to entire articles, in very special circumstances (for example, when an abstract's summary of key principles is succinct or quotable), you may want to cite only the abstract. In those rare instances, first prepare a full reference-list entry for the article; however, insert the word *Abstract*, not italicized, within brackets after the article's title. The period that normally follows the title follows the closing bracket.

McBride, M. E., Waldrop, W. B., Fehr, J. J., Boulet, J. R., & Murray, D. J. (2011). Simulation in pediatrics: The reliability and validity of a multiscenario assessment [Abstract]. *Pediatrics, 128*(2), 335–343. https://doi.org/10.154/peds.2010-3278d

   Parenthetical citation (McBride et al., 2011)

Shermer, L. O., Rose, K. C., & Hoffman, A. (2011). Perceptions and credibility: Understanding the nuances of eyewitness testimony [Abstract]. *Journal of Contemporary Justice, 27*(2), 183–203. https://doi.org/10.1177/1043986211405886

   Parenthetical citation (Shermer et al., 2011)

5c An Article in a Monthly Magazine

An article from a monthly magazine is listed by author. The date is given by year and month, separated by a comma, in parentheses. The article title appears next with sentence-style capitalization. The title of the magazine, with headline-style capitalization, is followed by a comma, the volume number, and the issue number; all but the issue number and the parentheses that enclose it are italicized. The entry ends with inclusive page numbers listed without a page abbreviation and a DOI or URL if one is available. Even though the month and year are included in a reference-list entry, only the year is included in the parenthetical citation.

Gorman, C. (2010, October). Closing the health gap. *Scientific American, 303*(4), 34, 36.

> ***Parenthetical citation*** (Gorman, 2010)

Notice that this article appears on nonconsecutive pages.

Madu, C. (2010, March–April). A cure for crime. *Psychology Today, 43*(2), 12.

> ***Parenthetical citation*** (Madu, 2010)

These two articles do not have DOIs; therefore, the entries end with page numbers.

5d An Article in a Weekly Magazine

The entry for a weekly magazine is identical to the entry for a monthly magazine except that the date of publication (along with the year and month) is included in parentheses. In the corresponding parenthetical citation, however, only the year is required.

Begley, S. (2010, February 8). The depressing news about antidepressants. *Newsweek, 155*(6), 34–41.

> ***Parenthetical citation*** (Begley, 2010)

Gibbs, N. (2011, March 21). Zero tolerance, zero sense. *Time, 177*(11), 62.

> ***Parenthetical citation*** (Gibbs, 2011)

5e An Article in a Newspaper

An entry for a newspaper article resembles that for a magazine, except that section numbers or letters are included.

When sections are indicated by letters, they are presented along with the page numbers, without intervening punctuation or space.

Pogrebin, R. (2010, April 22). A mother's loss, a daughter's story. *The New York Times*, E1, E9.

   Parenthetical citation (Pogrebin, 2010)

Notice that this article appears on nonconsecutive pages.

Sharma, A., Anand, G., Bahree, M., & Pokharel, K. (2011, July 3). The ailing health of a growing nation. *The Wall Street Journal*, A1, A10.

   Parenthetical citation (Sharma et al., 2011)

5f   An Article in a Newsletter

The entry for an article in a newsletter follows the pattern for a magazine: It includes the author, date, title of selection, title of newsletter, volume number, issue number, and inclusive pages (without page abbreviations). If a newsletter appears seasonally, include such identifying information along with the year (2012, Spring).

H1N1 pandemic vaccine safety: Results from clinical trials. (2010). *Immunization Newsletter*, 32(2), 5.

   Parenthetical citation ("H1N1," 2010)

An authorless article is cited by title. Notice that the shortened title is placed in quotation marks because the parenthetical note will appear in the text.

Kemp, P. M., Winecker, R. E., & Langman, L. J. (2011, July). A world of knowledge in forensic toxicology. *Academic News*, 41(4), 7, 34.

   Parenthetical citation (Kemp et al., 2011)

When pages are not sequential, list them all, separated by commas.

5g   An Editorial

The entry for an editorial—an opinion-based essay—resembles that for a magazine or newspaper article, with one exception: The word *Editorial* (not italicized) is placed within brackets immediately after the title of the essay, if there is one; if the editorial has no title, then the bracketed information appears on its own. The period that normally follows the title follows the closing bracket.

Cohen, R. (2012, December 7). Thanks for not sharing [Editorial]. *The New York Times*, 1.

   Parenthetical citation (Cohen, 2012)

Goti, J. M. (2010). A turbulent past and the problem of memory [Editorial]. *International Journal of Transitional Justice, 4*(2), 153–165. https://doi.org/10.1093/ijtj/ij9011

   Parenthetical citation (Goti, 2010)

5h A Letter to the Editor

Following the author's name and the publication date, include the title assigned to the letter (if one is provided) and the phrase *Letter to the editor* (not italicized) in brackets, followed by a period; if the letter to the editor has no title, then the bracketed information appears on its own. The rest of the entry follows the pattern appropriate for the periodical.

Kunisaki, C. (2011). [Letter to the editor]. *Journal of Surgical Oncology, 104*(3), 333. https://doi.org/10.1002/jso.21705

   Parenthetical citation (Kunisaki, 2011)

Large, M., & Ryan, C. J. (2012). Screening for suicide: A comment on Steeg et al. [Letter to the editor]. *Psychological Medicine, 42*(9), 2011–2012. https://doi.org/10.1017/s0033291712001377

   Parenthetical citation (Large & Ryan, 2012)

Notice that this letter to the editor has an attributed title.

5i A Review

After the author, date, and review title (if there is one), include a descriptive phrase that begins "Review of the book (film, music recording, car, computer game)" and ends with the specific product name; enclose this information in brackets, followed by a period. Then continue the entry as is appropriate for the source.

Earl, J. (2011). [Review of the book *Crimes of dissent: Civil disobedience, criminal justice, and the politics of conscience,* by J. S. Lovell]. *Law and Society, 45*(1), 224–225. https://doi.org/10.1111/j.1540-5893.2011.00433_2.x

   Parenthetical citation (Earl, 2011)

Rosen, D. (2012). [Review of the book *Improving medical outcomes: The psychology of doctor-patient visits,* by J. Leavitt & F. Leavitt]. *Journal of the American Medical Association, 307*(5), 514.

   Parenthetical citation (Rosen, 2012)

5j A Secondary Source

The authors of primary sources report their own research and ideas; the authors of secondary sources report the research and ideas of others. For example, in an article titled "Rationale and Evidence for Menu-Labeling Legislation" (*American Journal of Preventative Medicine*), Roberto, Schwartz, and Brownell (2009) reported on a study showing that federally mandated menu labeling at fast-food restaurants did, in fact, influence consumers to select foods with fewer calories; this article is considered a primary source. Yang and Nichols (2011) incorporated information and assessments from Roberto, Schwartz, and Brownell's original article in their article "Obesity and Health System Reform: Private vs. Public Responsibility"; Yang and Nichols's article is a secondary source. If the original or primary source (Roberto, Schwartz, & Brownell, 2009) is not available, use the secondary source (Yang & Nichols, 2011), following this sample.

Yang, Y. T., & Nichols, L. M. (2011). Obesity and health system reform: Private vs. public responsibility. *Journal of Law, Medicine, and Ethics*, *39*(3), 380–386. https://doi.org/10.1111/j.1748-720x.2011.0067.x

In-text commentary and parenthetical citation

Roberto, Schwartz, and Brownell (2009) observed that when menu labels are prominently displayed, customers will, with some regularity, select food with fewer calories (as cited in Yang & Nichols, 2011).

6 Citing Books and Other Separately Published Materials

Chapter Objectives:

- Learn to prepare reference-list entries for books and other separately published materials.
- Learn to prepare corresponding parenthetical citations for books and other separately published materials.
- Learn to arrange parenthetical citations when a reference list includes multiple works by the same author.
- Learn to distinguish between primary and secondary sources.

Reference-List Entries for Books and Other Separately Published Materials

6a A Book by One Author (86)
6b A Book by Two or More Authors (86)
6c A Book With No Author Named (87)
6d A Book With an Organization as Author (87)
6e An Edition Other Than the First (88)
6f An Edited Collection (88)
6g An Original Selection in an Edited Collection (88)
6h A Previously Published Selection in an Edited Collection (89)
6i A Revised or Enlarged Edition (90)
6j A Reprinted Book (90)
6k A Multivolume Work (90)
6l An Article in an Encyclopedia or Other Reference Work (91)
6m A Translation (92)
6n A Government Document—Committee, Commission, Department (92)
6o A Preface, Introduction, Foreword, Epilogue, or Afterword (93)
6p A Monograph (93)

(continued)

> **6q** A Pamphlet, Brochure, or Fact Sheet (94)
> **6r** An Unpublished Dissertation (94)
> **6s** Published Proceedings From a Conference (94)
> **6t** Multiple Works by the Same Author (95)
> **6u** A Secondary Source (96)

Books provide comprehensive, extended discussions of topics. Those published by scholarly or university presses are often targeted to specialists in particular fields and provide a broad range of technical information and complex analyses. Those published by trade (commercial) publishers are often directed to nonspecialists.

Because books take several years to produce, they frequently provide reflective interpretations that have the benefit of critical distance. Consequently, they provide balance in research.

With an increasing number of books (and other published materials) available in digital forms, APA now recommends including DOIs or URLs at the end of reference-list entries, if they are available. (See page 104 for a full discussion of how to include and format this element.)

To cite books in a reference list, follow the guidelines in this chapter.

6a A Book by One Author

The entry for a book by a single author begins with the author's name, followed by the year in parentheses, the title, and the publisher. A book title is presented in italics, with sentence-style capitalization.

Dickey, C. (2009). *Securing the city: Inside America's best counterterror force—the NYPD*. Simon.

   Parenthetical citation (Dickey, 2009)

Weiner, M. F. (2010). *Power, protest, and the public school: Jewish and African American struggles in New York City*. Rutgers University Press.

   Parenthetical citation (Weiner, 2010)

6b A Book by Two or More Authors

When a book has multiple authors, their names appear in the order presented on the title page, not alphabetical order. The names of two to twenty authors are listed, with all of their names inverted. An ampersand (&) joins the last two names. If a book has twenty-one or more authors, the first nineteen are listed, followed by ellipsis points (three spaced periods) and the name of the last author.

Lazarus, R. S., & Lazarus, B. N. (2006). *Coping with aging.* Oxford University Press.

Parenthetical citation (Lazarus & Lazarus, 2006)

Wright, J. P., Tibbetts, S. G., & Daigle, L. E. (2008). *Criminals in the making: Criminality across the life course.* Sage.

Parenthetical citation (Wright et al., 2008)

6c A Book With No Author Named

When no author or editor is named, list the book by title. When an editor is listed, begin with the editor's name. The following source is listed by title.

Federal regulatory directory: The essential guide to the history, organization, and impact of U.S. federal regulation (15th ed.). (2011). CQ Press–S. http://dx.doi.org/10.4135/9781483384757

Parenthetical citation (*Federal Regulatory Directory*, 2011)

Notice that the title is presented in headline-style capitalization in the parenthetical citation.

With an authorless book, the year follows the title or edition number. (See 6e for the common pattern of presenting editions.)

The following source is listed by editor.

VandenBos, G. R. (Ed.). (2007). *APA dictionary of psychology.* American Psychological Association. https://psycnet.apa.org/record/2006-11044-00

Parenthetical citation (VandenBos, 2007)

6d A Book With an Organization as Author

When an organization is listed as the author, spell out the name completely in the author position. When the organization is also the publisher, the name does not need to be repeated in the publisher position.

American Psychological Association. (2020). *Publication manual of the American Psychological Association* (7th ed.). https://doi.org/10.1037/0000165-000

First parenthetical citation (American Psychological Association [APA], 2020)

Subsequent citations (APA, 2020)

The first in-text citation with an organization as an author includes the full name, followed by the abbreviated name within brackets; additional references include only the abbreviated name.

American Hospital Association. (2011). *AHA guide to the health care field*. Health Forum.

   First parenthetical citation (American Hospital Association [AHA], 2011)

   Subsequent citations (AHA, 2011)

6e An Edition Other Than the First

The edition number, which appears on the title page, follows the title of the book, in parentheses. Note that it is not italicized and that the period that normally follows the title follows the closing parenthesis instead.

Moritsugu, J., Wong, F. Y., & Duffy, K. G. (2010). *Community psychology* (4th ed.). Allyn.

   Parenthetical citation (Moritsugu et al., 2010)

Long, L. L., & Young, M. E. (2007). *Counseling and therapy for couples* (2nd ed.). Brooks/Cole; Cengage.

   Parenthetical citation (Long & Young, 2007)

Note that dual publishers are both listed, separated by a semicolon.

6f An Edited Collection

Present an entire edited collection like a traditional book, with the editor's name in the author position.

Foreman, M. D., Milisen, K., & Fulner, T. T. (Eds.). (2010). *Critical care nursing of older adults: Best practices*. Springer.

   Parenthetical citation (Foreman et al., 2010)

Gilde, C. (Ed.). (2007). *Higher education: Open for business*. Lexington Books.

   Parenthetical citation (Gilde, 2007)

6g An Original Selection in an Edited Collection

To cite an original selection in an edited collection, begin with the name of the author of the selection, followed by the date in parentheses and the selection's title (with sentence-style capitalization and no quotation marks). Introduced by the word *In* (not italicized), the collection editor is listed next (the editor's name is in normal order, followed by the abbreviation *Ed.* in parentheses, not italicized), followed by a comma. The title of the collection, italicized, is followed by the inclusive page numbers for the selection, with the abbreviation for pages, listed in parentheses. The entry ends with the publisher and DOI or URL, if available.

Estrin, M., & Malm, C. (2010). State weakness and infectious diseases. In S. E. Rice, C. Graff, & C. Pascul (Eds.), *Confronting poverty: Weak states and U.S. national security* (pp. 167–201). Brookings Institution Press.

Parenthetical citation (Estrin & Malm, 2010)

Lurigio, A. J., & Snowden, J. (2008). Prison culture and the treatment and control of mentally ill offenders. In J. M. Bryne, D. Hummer, & F. S. Taxman (Eds.), *The culture of prison violence* (pp. 164–179). Prentice Hall.

Parenthetical citation (Lurigio & Snowden, 2008)

6h A Previously Published Selection in an Edited Collection

When a selection has been reprinted from a work published earlier, provide identifying information in parentheses at the end of the entry. Include the title of the original selection in quotation marks (even if it is the same), followed by the year of original publication, the title of the journal, volume and issue numbers, and inclusive pages. Note that brackets are used around the issue number (because the reprint information is already in parentheses). Then include a DOI or URL, if available, and insert a closing parenthesis. No period follows the closing parenthesis.

Bazemore, G., & Day, S. E. (2005). Restoring the balance: Juvenile and community justice. In D. L. Parry (Ed.), *Essential readings in juvenile justice* (pp. 405–414). Prentice Hall. (Reprinted from "Restoring the balance: Juvenile and community justice," 1996, *Juvenile Justice, 3*[1], 3–14)

Parenthetical citation (Bazemore & Day, 2005)

Soames, S. (2009). The necessary argument. In *Philosophical essays: Vol. 1. Natural language: What it means and how we use it* (pp. 202–207). Princeton University Press. (Reprinted from "The necessary argument," 1991, *Linguistics and Philosophy, 14,* 575–580)

Parenthetical citation (Soames, 2009)

This reprinted essay appears in the first volume of a multivolume work (see 6k).

6i A Revised or Enlarged Edition

Enclose the description of a revised or enlarged edition in parentheses following the title. As with other editions, the parenthetical information precedes the period that follows the title. This information is not italicized.

Houck, M. M., & Siegel, J. A. (2010). *Fundamentals of forensic science* (Rev. ed.). Academic Press. https://doi.org/10.1016/C2013-0-12985-6

   Parenthetical citation (Houck & Siegel, 2010)

Jacobs, L. R., & Skocpol, T. (2012). *Health care reform and American politics: What everyone needs to know* (Rev. ed.). Oxford University Press.

   Parenthetical citation (Jacobs & Skocpol, 2012)

6j A Reprinted Book

The entry for a reprinted book begins with the full entry of the version you have used; the entry ends with a parenthetical description of the original publication date, with no period after the closing parenthesis. Note that the parenthetical citation includes both dates, presented in chronological order, separated by a slash.

Kimmel, A. J. (2007). *Ethical issues in behavioral research: Basic and applied perspectives.* Wiley-Blackwell. (Original work published 1966)

   Parenthetical citation (Kimmel, 1966/2007)

Pritchard, E. W. (2009). *A complete report of the trial of Dr. E. W. Pritchard, for the alleged poisoning of his wife and mother-in-law.* General Books. (Original work published 1865)

   Parenthetical citation (Pritchard, 1865/2009)

6k A Multivolume Work

When citing a complete multivolume work, the number of volumes appears in parentheses following the title but before the period; if an edition number is required, it precedes the volume number.

Fisher, B. S., & Lab, S. P. (Eds.). (2010). *Encyclopedia of victimology and crime prevention* (Vols. 1–2). Sage Publications.

Parenthetical citation (Fisher & Lab, 2010)

When citing a separately titled volume of a multivolume work, list the multivolume title first, followed by a colon and one space. Then list the separate volume number, followed by a period, and the single volume title. The multivolume title, volume information, and specific title are all italicized. Note that the names of series editors precede those of volume editors; the order of presentation, then, corresponds to the order of the titles.

Boon, K. E., Huq, A., & Lovelace, D. C. (Vol. Eds). (2011). *Terrorism: Commentary on security documents: Vol. 116. Assessing President Obama's national security strategy*. Oxford University Press.

Parenthetical citation (Boon et al., 2011)

61 An Article in an Encyclopedia or Other Reference Work

To cite an article in an encyclopedia or other reference work, begin with the author's name, when it is available, followed by the date in parentheses. Next list the subject heading under which the material appears (exactly as it appears in the source), without special punctuation. Follow it with the title of the reference work. In parentheses, but before the period that follows the title, include the volume number, if applicable, and inclusive page numbers. End the entry with the publisher.

When a reference work has a large editorial board, include the first editor's name and *et al.* (not italicized) to substitute for the other editors' names.

Barber, C. (2009). Gender identity. In E. M. Anderman & L. H. Anderman (Eds.), *Psychology of classroom learning: An encyclopedia* (Vols. 1–2, pp. 428–430). Gale; Cengage. https://doi.org/10.1108/09504120911003203

Parenthetical citation (Barber, 2009)

Sulloway, F. J. (2007). Birth order and sibling competition. In R. I. M. Dunbar & L. Barrett (Eds.), *Oxford handbook of evolutionary psychology* (pp. 297–311). Oxford University Press.

Parenthetical citation (Sulloway, 2007)

6m A Translation

Under most circumstances, the translator of a text is cited in parentheses immediately after the title of the selection (whether it is an essay, chapter, or complete text) but before the closing period for that element.

de Beauvoir, S. (2003). The married woman (H. M. Parshly, Trans.). In S. Hirschberg & T. Hirschberg (Eds.), *Past to present: Ideas that changed our world* (pp. 188–194). Prentice Hall.

   Parenthetical citation (de Beauvoir, 2003)

The previous example indicates that Parshly translated only the selection presented in this entry. Had he translated the entire collection, his name would have appeared after the anthology's title.

Nietzsche, F. (2011). *Beyond good and evil* (H. Zimmern, Trans.). Tribeca Books. (Original work published 1886)

   Parenthetical citation (Nietzsche, 1886/2011)

This entry indicates that Zimmern translated the entire book.

6n A Government Document—Committee, Commission, Department

An entry for a government document follows the pattern used for another similar source. Because many government documents are book-length, that pattern most often applies. Note, however, that APA style requires a publication number for a government document, if available (usually found on the title page or back cover), to be presented in parentheses after the title; the document number is not italicized.

Root, E. D., Allpress, J. L., Cajka, J. C., Lambert, S. B., Savitz, L. A., & Bernard, S. L. (2007). *Emergency preparedness atlas: U.S. nursing home and hospital facilities* (AHRHS 07–0029–2). Agency of Healthcare Research and Quality–U.S. Department of Health and Human Services. https://www.hsdl.org/view&did=478074

   Parenthetical citation (Root et al., 2007)

Scaperlanda, M. A. (2009). *Immigration law: A primer*. Federal Judicial Center. https://www.fjc.gov/sites/default/files/2012/ImmLaw09.pdf

   Parenthetical citation (Scaperlanda, 2009)

6o A Preface, Introduction, Foreword, Epilogue, or Afterword

When introductory or closing material is titled, it is presented like a selection in a collection; however, a descriptive word (*Preface, Epilogue*, and so on, not italicized) is enclosed within brackets before the period. Cite pages as they appear in the source, using either lowercase Roman or Arabic numerals.

Untitled material is cited separately by providing a descriptive title (within brackets), followed by complete entry information.

Kassel, J. D., & Veilleux, J. C. (2010). The complex interplay between substance abuse and emotion [Introduction]. In J. D. Kassel (Ed.), *Substance abuse and emotion* (pp. 3–12). American Psychological Association. https://doi.org/10.1037/12067-000

Parenthetical citation (Kassel & Veilleux, 2010)

Nieto, S. (2007). The national mythology and urban teaching [Introduction]. In G. Campano, *Immigrant students and literacy: Reading, writing, and remembering* (pp. 1–6). Teachers College Press.

Parenthetical citation (Nieto, 2007)

6p A Monograph

To create an entry for a monograph (a separately published, essay-length selection that is sometimes a reprint of a journal article and sometimes an independently prepared selection), include traditional publishing information. However, after the title and in brackets, include the monograph series title for clarity and monograph number, if available; the monograph number is introduced by *No.*, the abbreviation for *number*.

Brown, R., & Stobart, K. (2008). *Understanding boundaries and containment in clinical practice* [Society of Analytical Psychology Monograph]. Karnac.

Parenthetical citation (Brown & Stobart, 2008)

Ginsburg, J., Taylor, T., & Barr, M. S. (2009). *Nurse practitioners in primary care* [A Policy Monograph of the American College of Physicians]. American College of Physicians. https://www.acponline.org/system/files/documents/advocacy/current_policy_papers/assets/np_pc.pdf

Parenthetical citation (Ginsburg et al., 2009)

6q A Pamphlet, Brochure, or Fact Sheet

When a pamphlet, brochure, or fact sheet contains clearly presented information about author, date, and publisher, it is cited like a book, with a descriptive title enclosed in brackets. When information is missing, use these abbreviations: *n.p.* for "no publisher" and *n.d.* for "no date." None of these abbreviations is italicized in an entry.

Office of Victim Assistance. (2010). *Children affected by crime* [Brochure].

> **First parenthetical citation** (Office of Victim Assistance [OVA], 2010)
>
> **Subsequent citations** (OVA, 2010)

VA Research on Traumatic brain injury [Fact Sheet]. (2012). U.S. Department of Veteran Affairs.

> **Parenthetical citation** (*VA Research on Traumatic Brain Injury*, 2012)

In the parenthetical citation, headline-style capitalization is used.

6r An Unpublished Dissertation

A published dissertation is a book and should be cited accordingly (see 6a). The entry for an unpublished dissertation begins with the author's name, the date, and the title, presented in the pattern used for a book. In brackets, include the phrase *Unpublished doctoral dissertation* (not italicized), followed by a period. Then provide the name of the degree-granting university.

Sherriff, G. L. R. (2010). *Stranger than fiction: True crime narratives in contemporary Latin American literature*. [Unpublished doctoral dissertation]. Yale University.

> **Parenthetical citation** (Sherriff, 2010)

Sperstad, R. A. (2010). *Nursing education: Cultural transformation through guided critical reflection*. [Unpublished doctoral dissertation]. University of St. Thomas.

> **Parenthetical citation** (Sperstad, 2010)

6s Published Proceedings From a Conference

The published proceedings from a conference present revised, printed versions of papers that were delivered at the meeting. If the proceedings are published individually, cite them as books. If they are published regularly, present them as periodicals.

Holtman, B. (2011). Future challenges and new actors: From crime prevention to safe communities. In *Proceedings of ICPC's 15th anniversary conference: Crime prevention across the world: Taking stock, evaluation, and future perceptions* [Conference proceedings] (pp. 72–82). International Centre for the Prevention of Crime.

Parenthetical citation (Holtman, 2011)

Keyserling, H. (2011, February 23–24). Immunization of healthcare personnel. In *First international conference on measles immunization* [Conference proceedings] (pp. 57–67). Centers for Disease Control and Prevention.

Parenthetical citation (Keyserling, 2011)

6t Multiple Works by the Same Author

When citing several sources by the same author, repeat the name completely each time. Alphabetical order takes precedence, with single authors listed before multiple authors. List works by single authors or by the same multiple authors chronologically. If works are published in the same year, arrange them alphabetically by title.

Sternberg, R. J. (1990). *Metaphors of the mind: Conceptions of the nature of intelligence*. Cambridge University Press.

Sternberg, R. J. (Ed.). (2003). *Psychologists defying the crowd: Stories of those who battled the establishment and won*. American Psychological Association.

Sternberg, R. J. (2003). *Why smart people can be so stupid*. Yale University Press.

Sternberg, R. J. (2007). *Wisdom, intelligence, and creativity synthesized*. Cambridge University Press.

Sternberg, R. J., & Grigorenko, E. L. (2003). *The psychology of abilities, competencies, and expertise*. Cambridge University Press.

Sternberg, R. J., & Grigorenko, E. L. (2007). *Teaching for successful intelligence: To increase student learning and achievement* (2nd ed.). Corwin Press.

Sternberg, R. J., & Preiss, D. D. (Eds.). (2005). *Intelligence and technology: The impact of tools on the nature and development of human abilities*. Routledge.

Alternative parenthetical citations

The 1990 book: (Sternberg, 1990)

The first 2003 book: (Sternberg, 2003a)

The second 2003 book: (Sternberg, 2003b)

All four single-author works in the same citation: (Sternberg, 1990, 2003a, 2003b, 2007)

The first multiple-author book: (Sternberg & Grigorenko, 2003)

The second multiple-author book: (Sternberg & Grigorenko, 2007)

The third multiple-author book: (Sternberg & Preiss, 2005)

A combination of sources in the same citation: (Sternberg, 1990, 2007; Sternberg & Grigorenko, 2003)

Sternberg's four separately written works appear first, arranged in chronological order; the two 2003 books are arranged alphabetically by title. The Sternberg and Grigorenko books follow, also in chronological order. The Sternberg and Preiss book is last.

6u A Secondary Source

The authors of primary sources report their own research and ideas; the authors of secondary sources report the research and ideas of others. For example, Fisher, Bynum, and Skinner (2009) reported on hospitals' financial practices in an article titled "Getting Past Denial: The High Cost of Health Care in the United States" (*New England Journal of Medicine*); it is a primary source. Aries and Caress (2011) incorporated material from Fisher, Bynum, and Skinner's article in their book chapter "Hospitals: The Power of Institutional Interests"; the chapter is, consequently, a secondary source for the material. If the original or primary source (Fisher, Bynum, & Skinner, 2009) is unavailable, use the secondary source (Aries & Caress, 2011), following the pattern below.

Aries, N., & Caress, B. (2011). Hospitals: The power of institutionalized interests. In D. M. Nickitas, D. J. Middaugh, & N. Aries (Eds.), *Policy and politics for nurses and other health professionals* (pp. 123–141). Jones.

In-text commentary and parenthetical citation

Fisher, Bynum, and Skinner (2009) observed that to remain viable, hospitals must both integrate their systems and find additional ways to lower costs (as cited in Aries & Caress, 2011).

7 Citing Audiovisual Sources

Chapter Objectives:

- Learn to prepare reference-list entries for audiovisual sources.
- Learn to prepare corresponding parenthetical citations for audiovisual sources.

Reference-List Entries for Audiovisual Sources

7a A Film (97)
7b A Slide Set or Filmstrip (98)
7c A Television Broadcast (98)
7d A Radio Broadcast (99)
7e A Recording (99)
7f An Interview (100)
7g A Lecture or Speech (101)
7h A Work of Art (101)
7i A Map, Graph, Table, or Chart (101)

Audiovisual sources—films, recordings, speeches, works of art, and other visual images—are used infrequently in APA papers. Nevertheless, they can provide interesting support for discussions and create variety within a paper.

To cite an audiovisual source in a reference list, follow the guidelines in this chapter.

7a A Film

An entry for a film begins with the director's name (with the word *Director* in parentheses but not italicized), followed by the year of the film's release, its title (italicized, with sentence-style capitalization), and a descriptive title (in brackets). The entry ends with the name of the production company.

To highlight the work of individuals associated with the film, you may include their roles and names in brackets after the title, using brief phrases (*Narr. by, With, Written by*—not italicized).

Russell, D. O. (Director). (2012). *Silver linings playbook* [Film]. [With B. Cooper, J. Lawrence, R. De Niro, & J. Weaver]. The Weinstein Company; Mirage Enterprises.

> **Parenthetical citation** (Russell, 2012)

Lary, B. K. (Director). (2008). *History of world criminal justice* [Film]. [Written by B. K. Lary, A. Carlton, & M. Westin]. Insight Media.

> **Parenthetical citation** (Lary, 2008)

7b A Slide Set or Filmstrip

A slide set (either photographic slides or those prepared in PowerPoint or other digital formats) or a filmstrip is cited just as a film is, with one exception: Include a descriptive title, such as *Slide set*, in brackets (but not italicized) after the title.

Determined accord: Pandemic preparedness workshop for community managers [Slide set]. (2009). U.S. Department of Homeland Security; Federal Emergency Management Agency.

> **Parenthetical citation** (*Determined Accord*, 2009)

Because the source had no producer or director, the citation begins with the title. The parenthetical citation uses a shortened version of the title.

Technical Working Group for Eyewitness Evidence. (2003). *Eyewitness evidence: A trainer's manual for law enforcement* (NCJ 188678) [Slides]. U.S. Department of Justice.

> **First parenthetical citation** (Technical Working Group for Eyewitness Evidence [TWGEE], 2003)
>
> **Subsequent citations** (TWGEE, 2003)

As a government document, this entry incorporates a publication number after the title of the slide series.

7c A Television Broadcast

A regular television program is listed by executive producer, broadcast date (which may be either a single year or a set of inclusive dates to indicate the entire run of the program), program title (italicized, with sentence-style capitalization), a descriptive phrase (in brackets), and the name of the production company. If you want to include other people's contributions, list them after the program title (in brackets), using brief phrases (*Narr. by, With, Written by*—not italicized) to clarify their roles.

Grammer, K., Casey, P., Lee, D., Angell, D., & Lloyd, C. (Executive Producers). (1993–2004). *Frazier* [TV series]. Grub Street Productions; Paramount Television; Grammet Productions.

Parenthetical citation (Grammer et al., 1993–2004)

To refer to an individual episode, cite the writer and director, the specific broadcast date, the episode title (with sentence-style capitalization but without special punctuation), the season number and episode number (in parentheses), and a descriptive phrase in brackets. Introduced by the word *In* (not italicized), the series' executive producer is listed next (the producer's name is in normal order, followed by the phrase *Executive Producer* in parentheses, not italicized), followed by a comma. The title of the series follows, along with other standard information.

Cassidy, S. (Writer), & Letterman, J. (Director). (2019, November 5). Good Soldiers (Season 2, Episode 7) [TV series episode]. In D. Foster, A. Ginsburg, P. Horton, Y. S. Razack, D. Schular, & M. Slovis (Executive Producers), *New Amsterdam*. Pico Creek Productions; Universal Television.

Parenthetical citation (Cassidy & Letterman, 2019)

Note that only the year appears in the parenthetical citation.

7d A Radio Broadcast

An entry for a radio broadcast follows the guidelines for a television broadcast; however, note that a radio station's call letters or call numbers are listed. When a broadcast does not have an assigned title, add a descriptive phrase in brackets.

Balancing work, medication, and mental illness [Radio broadcast]. (2012, January 30). In *Talk of the nation*. NPR.

Parenthetical citation ("Balancing Work," 2012)

Silberner, J. (2011, September 5). Chronic fatigue syndrome still a medical mystery [Radio broadcast]. In *Morning edition*. NPR.

Parenthetical citation (Silberner, 2011)

7e A Recording

An entry for an entire recording begins with the recording artist's name, the date of the recording, and the album title (in italics, with sentence-style capitalization), with the word *Album*, not italicized, in brackets; although not required, you can also include the recording format after a semicolon. The entry ends with the name of the record label.

Winehouse, A. (2006). *Back to black* [Album; CD]. Universal Records.

> **Parenthetical citation** (Winehouse, 2006)

To emphasize a single selection on a recording, begin with the name of the recording artist and the date, followed by the title of the individual selection (with sentence-style capitalization but without special punctuation). Using the word *On* (not italicized), include the title of the complete recording and other production information. For additional clarity, you may include the track number in the parenthetical citation.

The Beatles. (2009). Helter skelter. [Written by P. McCartney]. On *The white album* (Remastered) [Album; CD]. Capital; EMI. (Original work released 1968)

> **Parenthetical citation** (The Beatles, 1968/2009, disc 2, track 6)

For clarity, the composer's name has been added, in brackets, after the song title. A remastered recording, like a revised or reprinted book, requires clarification in parentheses, as well as a parenthetical statement about the original release. Both release dates are included in the parenthetical citation, separated by a slash.

A classical recording begins with the composer's name in the "author" position; following the title, in brackets, include the phrase *Album recorded by* (not italicized) and the name of the performer or performers.

7f An Interview

An interview is a personal communication. As such, it is not included in a reference list. However, it is cited parenthetically in the text of the paper by enclosing the name of the person who was interviewed, the phrase *personal communication* (not italicized), and the date in parentheses. Notice that initials are required with the name.

> Although "correctional education" once meant providing the incarcerated with comprehensive educational experiences (including college-level courses), the current trend is to provide only vocational training; while expedient and cost effective, this shift of focus is extremely short-sighted (L. R. Bates, personal communication, August 16, 2019).

7g A Lecture or Speech

An entry for a lecture or speech (as well as other kinds of spoken public presentations) includes the speaker's name, the date of the speech, the title of the speech with sentence-style capitalization (italicized), and a descriptive title (in brackets). Then information about the speech-making context (the name of the conference or lecture series, along with the city, state, and country) is included.

Stevens, J. P. (2011, October 11). *A conversation with Justice John Paul Stevens* [Lecture and Discussion]. Public Lecture Series, Princeton University, Princeton, NJ, United States.

Parenthetical citation (Stevens, 2011)

Volkow, N. (2011, April 25). *The neurobiology of drug addiction*. [Lecture]. Public Lecture Series, Princeton University, Princeton, NJ, United States.

Parenthetical citation (Volkow, 2011)

7h A Work of Art

An entry for a work of art includes the artist's name, the completion date, the title assigned by the artist (italicized), a description of the medium (enclosed in brackets), the name of the museum or collection, and the city, state, and country where the museum is located. When an artist has not assigned a title to a work, include a brief description in brackets.

Hopper, E. (1930). *Early Sunday morning* [Oil on canvas]. Whitney Museum of American Art, New York, NY, United States.

Parenthetical citation (Hopper, 1930)

Warhol, A. (1964). *Electric chair* [Screenprint and acrylic on canvas]. Tate Modern, London, England.

Parenthetical citation (Warhol, 1964)

7i A Map, Graph, Table, or Chart

Often prepared as part of another source, a map, graph, table, or chart is most often treated like a selection in an edited collection (or a chapter in a book). If known, include the name of the author, artist, or designer responsible for the element, followed by the publication date, in parentheses. Include the title, with sentence-style capitalization but without special punctuation. Follow the title with a descriptive label in brackets, followed by a period. Then include entry information required for the source.

When a map, graph, table, or chart is prepared independently, it is treated like a book.

Federal Bureau of Investigation. (2010). Arrests by race, 2006 [Table]. In S. L. Gabbidon, *Race, ethnicity, crime, and justice: An international dilemma* (pp. 74–77). Sage.

First parenthetical citation (Federal Bureau of Investigation [FBI], 2010)

Subsequent citations (FBI, 2010)

Pérez, M. A., & Luquis, R. R. (2008). U.S. population by state, density, and distribution, 2006 [Map]. In M. A. Pérez & R. R. Luquis (Eds.), *Cultural competence in health education and health promotion* (p. 4). Jossey-Bass.

Parenthetical citation (Pérez & Luquis, 2008)

8 Citing Electronic Sources

Chapter Objectives:

- Learn to prepare reference-list entries for electronic sources.
- Learn to prepare corresponding parenthetical citations for electronic sources.

Reference-List Entries for Electronic Sources

8a An Article in an Online Journal (106)
8b An Article in an Online Magazine (106)
8c An Article in an Online Newspaper (106)
8d An Article in an Online Newsletter (107)
8e An Online Book (107)
8f An Online Dissertation or Thesis (108)
8g An Online Abstract (108)
8h An Article in an Online Encyclopedia or Other Reference Work (109)
8i A Website or Scholarly Project (109)
8j An Online Transcript of a Lecture or Speech (110)
8k An Online Map, Graph, Table, or Chart (110)
8l A CD-ROM Source (111)
8m An Email Interview (111)
8n An Online Video (112)
8o An Audio Podcast (112)
8p A Posting—Blog, Discussion Group, Facebook, or Twitter (113)

The internet provides researchers with access to an amazing array of resources. Many periodicals are now available in electronic, as well as print, form. Books—out-of-print volumes, as well as recent publications—are accessible online. Documents, correspondence, photographs, films, recordings, and a host of other resource materials are available online in digitized form. Because these sources are available anywhere that a researcher can establish an internet connection, research is no longer a local activity, restricted to a nearby library, lab, or collection. Instead, researchers can access a far broader range of materials than they once could.

Take advantage of the wealth of online material but be aware that citing these resources sometimes requires ingenuity because citation information can be difficult to locate.

To cite online sources in a reference list, follow the guidelines in this chapter.

Principles for Citing Electronic Sources

1. **Follow patterns for similar print sources when possible.** Use reference-list entries for similar print sources as your guide: Include as much of the information that is required for corresponding print versions as you can locate and present the information in the same order and format.

2. **Use a digital object identifier (DOI) when available.** Current publications usually display the DOI—a fixed alphanumeric link to an online document—at the top of the first page. When it is available, use it to identify the source.

3. **Use a uniform resource locator (URL) as an alternative.** When a DOI is not available, use the URL of your specific source, not the URL of the website's home page.

4. **Present a source's DOI or URL with care.** To ensure that you record a DOI or URL exactly, copy and paste it into your reference-list entry.

5. **Divide the DOI or URL when advised to do so.** APA recommends leaving DOIs and URLs intact. However, if your instructor directs you to, divide the number and letter sequences *after* punctuation to avoid unusually large blank spaces in reference-list entries; however, retain *http://* or *https://* as a unit.

6. **Retain hyperlinks or eliminate them, according to your instructor's recommendation.** Hyperlinks (http:// or https://) take readers directly to the material that you have referenced. If your paper is being submitted online, then retaining these links (represented with a blue font and underlining) is probably a good choice; with one click, a reader will be taken to your source. However, if your paper is being printed, turning off the hyperlink feature is a reasonable option; DOIs and URLs will remain in your entries, but without the distracting blue font and underlining (which seems to be a link but actually isn't).

Citing Electronic Sources

Either strategy is acceptable, but follow the recommendations of your instructor and be consistent.

As you gather information to cite electronic sources, your goal should be to provide the most complete set of information possible for each electronic source.

Specialized Online Sources

Online sources exist in many forms. Although they are all designed in approximately the same way—with a home page that directs users to subpages where information can be found—some specialized sites have distinct purposes and applications.

- **Websites.** Websites affiliated with professional organizations provide materials that support or enhance the work of the organization—research documents, online resources, web links, news items, press releases, and so on. Website titles typically include the organization's name, but if they do not, this information may be added for clarity. Other websites are developed by a broad range of entities: universities, businesses, government agencies, museums, institutes, and even individuals; these sites serve a variety of specific (and not always academic) purposes.

- **Information databases.** Typically developed by information-technology firms or governmental agencies, these sites provide access to cataloged information that is accessed by using keyword search terms. Periodical databases like ProQuest, EBSCOhost, LexisNexis, JSTOR, and WorldCat make periodical articles available in a variety of formats; other databases provide access to cataloged recordings, images, historical documents, and so on. Because these databases direct you to original documents that are often accessible through various means, APA no longer requires that databases be included in reference-list entries.

- **Scholarly projects.** Often affiliated with universities, foundations, and government agencies, these sites are depositories of resources as varied as articles, books, digitized images of original documents, sound recordings, and film clips. Because their affiliations help establish their credibility, that information is sometimes included in reference-list entries.

8a An Article in an Online Journal

Some online journals reproduce what is also available in a complementary print version; however, some journals are available only in an online format, which may or may not contain all of the elements from a print journal (numbered paging, for example). To cite an article in an online journal, first provide as much of the information that is required for the print version of the article as is available (see 5a). End the entry with the article's DOI, if one is available. Otherwise, use the specific URL for the article.

Orth, U., Trzesniewski, K. H., & Robbins, R. W. (2010). Self-esteem development from young adulthood to old age: A cohort-sequential longitudinal study. *Journal of Personality and Social Psychology*, *98*(4), 645–658. https://doi.org/10.1037/a0018769

  Parenthetical citation (Orth et al., 2010)

Yehia, B., & Frank, I. (2011). Battling AIDS in America: An evaluation of the national HIV/AIDS strategy. *American Journal of Public Health*, *111*(9), E4–E8. https://doi.org/10.2105/AJPH.2011.300259

  Parenthetical citation (Yehia & Frank, 2011)

8b An Article in an Online Magazine

To cite an article in an online magazine, provide as much of the required information for the print version as is available (see 5c and 5d). End the entry with the article's DOI, if available, or the specific URL.

Fitzpatrick, L. (2010, February 23). The death penalty: Racist, classist, and unfair. *Time*. http://content.time.com/time/nation/article/0,8599,1967233,00.html

  Parenthetical citation (Fitzpatrick, 2010)

Miller, G. (2010, May). How our brains make memories. *Smithsonian*, *41*(2), 38–45. https://smithsonianmag.com/science-nature/how-our-brains-make-memories-14466850/

  Parenthetical citation (Miller, 2010)

8c An Article in an Online Newspaper

To cite an article in an online newspaper, first provide the information that is required for the print version of the article, if it is available (see 5e). End the entry with the article's DOI, if available, or the specific URL.

Dance, A. (2011, August 22). Therapeutic hypothermia: Keeping cool in emergencies. *Los Angeles Times Online*. https://latimes.com/health/la-xpm-2011-aug-22-la-he-therapeutic-cooling-20110822-story.html

Parenthetical citation (Dance, 2011)

Hax, C. (2012, December 11). Working up the courage to get counseling for depression. *The Washington Post*. https://washingtonpost.com/lifestyle/style/working-up-the-courage-to-get-counseling-for-depression/2012/12/10/4b56c00e-38fa-11e2-b01f-5f55b193f58f_story.html

Parenthetical citation (Hax, 2012)

8d An Article in an Online Newsletter

An entry for an online newsletter follows the same pattern as that for an online newspaper (see 5f). End the entry with the article's DOI, if available, or the specific URL.

Higgins, E. (2019, December 5). The dangerous narrative that lurks under the "achievement gap." *Education Week*. https://www.edweek.org/ew/articles/2019/12/06/the-dangerous-narrative-that-lurks-under-the.html?cmp=eml-enl-eu-news3&M=%%MESSAGE_ID%%&U=%%CF_ICNACCOUNTNUMBER%%&UUID=%%MD5_EMAIL%%

Parenthetical citation (Higgins, 2019)

Waking up to anesthesia: Learning more before you go under. (2011, April). *NIH News in Health*. https://newsinhealth.nih.gov/2011/04/waking-up-anesthesia

Parenthetical citation ("Waking Up," 2011)

8e An Online Book

To cite an online book, first prepare a standard entry (see 6a to 6r); however, omit the publisher. Then include the name of the online source and the DOI, if available, or the specific URL.

Pierce, R. V. (1895). *The people's common sense medical advisor in plain English, or medicine simplified* (54th ed.). Project Gutenberg. https://gutenberg.org/files/18467/18467-h/advise.html

Parenthetical citation (Pierce, 1895)

Treverton, G. F. (2008). *Reorganizing U.S. domestic intelligence: Assessing the options* (Rand Monographs). Rand Corporation; Homeland Security Program; The Intelligence Policy Center. https://rand.org/content/dam/rand/pubs/monographs/2008/RAND_MG767.pdf

Parenthetical citation (Treverton, 2008)

8f An Online Dissertation or Thesis

A dissertation or thesis may be accessed through a database such as ProQuest or may be accessed from institutional archives; the format is distinct depending on the source.

If using a database, begin with author, date, and title, followed by the publication number in parentheses; after one space include (in brackets) the phrase *Doctoral dissertation* or *Master's thesis* (not italicized) and the degree-granting university; the closing bracket is followed by a period. Then provide the name of the database.

If you gained access online, begin with the author, date, and title; in brackets, include the phrase *Doctoral dissertation* or *Master's thesis* (not italicized) and the name of the degree-granting university; the closing bracket is followed by a period. End the entry with the source (most likely a university archive) and a URL.

Blandon, K. C. (2011). Brain, psyche, and self: A dialectic between analytic psychology and neuroscience (Publication No. 3519792) [Doctoral dissertation, Pacifica Graduate Institute]. ProQuest Dissertations and Theses Global.

Parenthetical citation (Blandon, 2011)

Betzel, R. F. (2015). Age-related changes in human anatomical and functional brain networks [Doctoral dissertation, Indiana University—Bloomington]. IU ScholarWorks. https://scholarworks.iu.edu/dspace/handle/2022/20388

Parenthetical citation (Betzel, 2015)

8g An Online Abstract

To cite an abstract of an article in an online journal or an abstract from an online service, first provide the information that is required for the print version of an abstract (see 5b). End the entry with the DOI, if available, or the specific URL.

Der Pau, P. J., Deng, L. F., Chang, S. S. H., & Jiang, K. T. (2011). Correctional officers' perceptions of a solution-focused training program: Potential implications for working with offenders

[Abstract]. *International Journal of Offender Therapy and Comparative Criminology, 55,* 863–879. https://journals.sagepub.com/doi/10.1177/0306624X10378231

Parenthetical citation (Der Pau et al., 2011)

Woodhead, E. L., Chin-Newman, C., Spink, K., Hoang, M., & Smith, S. A. (2020, January 16). College students' disclosure of mental health problems on campus [Abstract]. *Journal of American College Health.* Advance online publication. https://tandfonline.com/doi/full/10.1080/07448481.2019.1706533

Parenthetical citation (Woodhead et al., 2020)

8h An Article in an Online Encyclopedia or Other Reference Work

To cite an article from an online encyclopedia or reference work, first provide the information required for a print source (see 6l). End the entry with the DOI, if available, or the specific URL.

Intelligence. (2020). In *APA dictionary of psychology.* https://dictionary-apa.org/intelligence

Parenthetical citation ("Intelligence," 2020)

Karmen, A. (2020). Victimology. In *Brittanica encyclopedia online.* https://britannica.com/topic/victimology

Parenthetical citation (Karmen, 2020)

8i A Website or Scholarly Project

If you refer to an entire website or scholarly project, you do not need to include an entry in your reference list. However, you must identify the title of the source clearly in the text of your paper (capitalized but without special punctuation) and provide the electronic address in parentheses, as in this sample:

> In addition to membership services, the American Psychological Association website includes several extremely useful subpages for general readers—including "News & Events," which lists meetings and includes APA-related news releases; "Topics," which addresses subjects ranging from ADHD to workplace issues; and "Psychological Help Center," which provides brief articles, lists of suggestions, and blogs (http://www.apa.org).

To cite a source—an article, illustration, map, or other element—from a website or scholarly project, include the author (or artist, compiler, or editor) of the individual source, if available;

the date; and the title of the source, italicized. Then include the name of the website (capitalized but without italics) and the URL for the individual element.

Dettman, L. (2017, November). *Fumes across the fence line: The health impacts of air pollution from oil and gas facilities on African American communities*. NAACP. http://naacp.org/wp-content/uploads/2017/11/Fumes-Across-the-Fence-Line_NAACP-and-CATF-Study.pdf

    Parenthetical citation (Dettman, 2017)

Treating opiod addiction in criminal justice settings. (2017, December). National Institute on Drug Abuse. https://drugabuse.gov/publications/treating-opioid-addiction-in-criminal-justice-settings/treating-opioid-addiction-in-criminal-justice-settings

    Parenthetical citation ("Treating Opiod Addiction," 2017)

8j   An Online Transcript of a Lecture or Speech

To cite an online transcript of a lecture or speech, include the speaker's name, the date, and the title, italicized (or a description, not italicized, in brackets). Then include the phrase *Speech Transcript*, not italicized and in brackets. End the entry with the source and the DOI or URL.

Darrow, C. (1924, August 22). [Summary defense for Leopold & Loeb]. [Speech transcript]. Voices of America. https://voicesofdemocracy.umd.edu/clarence-darrow-plea-for-leopold-and-loeb-22-23-and-25-august-1924-speech-text/

    Parenthetical citation (Darrow, 1924)

Johnson, L. B. (1965, July 30). [Remarks at the signing of the Medicare Bill, Independence, MO] [Speech transcript]. LBJ Presidential Library. http://lbjlibrary.net/collections/selected-speeches/1965/07-30-1965.html

    Parenthetical citation (Johnson, 1965)

Because these speeches have no formal title, a descriptive phrase is added in brackets; notice that the period follows the description. If a speech has a title, it is italicized.

8k   An Online Map, Graph, Table, or Chart

To cite an online map, graph, table, or chart, first provide the information required for the kind of visual element (see 7i). End the entry with the DOI or URL.

Centers for Disease Control and Prevention. (2019, February 21). Tobacco product use among high school students—2018 [Table]. https://cdc.gov/vitalsigns/youth-tobacco-use/

First parenthetical citation (Centers for Disease Control and Prevention [CDC], 2011)

Subsequent citations (CDC, 2011)

Although logic might suggest that the acronym would be *CDCP*, the organization continues to use the older, shorter, more familiar form: *CDC*.

United States Geological Survey. (2020, January). Years vs. acres burned [1955–2020] [Chart]. https://wim.usgs.gov/geonarrative/firescience/

First parenthetical citation (United States Geological Survey [USGS], 2020)

Subsequent citations (USGS, 2020)

8l A CD-ROM Source

To cite a CD-ROM source, include the author or editor, the release date, and the title, italicized, followed by a description of the format in brackets.

Department of Health and Human Services. (2013, July 31). *National health interview survey*, 1993 [CD-ROM]. https://hdl.handle.net/1902.29/CD-11487

First parenthetical citation (Department of Health and Human Services [DHHS], 2013)

Subsequent citations (DHHS, 2013)

Schmalleger, F. T. (2008). *Criminal justice simulations* (10th ed.) [CD-ROM]. Prentice Hall.

Parenthetical citation (Schmalleger, 2008)

8m An Email Interview

An interview conducted through email correspondence is considered personal communication. As such, it is not included in the reference list. However, it is cited in the text of the paper by enclosing the phrase *personal communication* (not italicized) and the date of the email in parentheses.

Marshall (personal communication, September 9, 2019) noted that while electronic diagnostics can improve record keeping, patients often resent clinicians keying in data during consultations.

8n An Online Video

To cite a video, include the person or group that posted the video, followed by the posting date. Next, include the title of the video (using sentence-style capitalization, without italics); in brackets, place the word *Video* (not italicized), followed by a period. Then identify the source and the URL.

You may provide additional information about the film (director, writer, performers, and so on) in brackets for clarity, following the patterns used for regularly distributed films (see 7a).

Rich, J. (2010, January 6). *Wrong place, wrong time: Understanding trauma and violence in the lives of young black men* [Video]. National Institutes of Health. https://videocast/nih.gov/watch=8230

   Parenthetical citation (Rich, 2010)

World Health Organization. (2012). *What's disability to me? Faustina's story* [Video]. https://who.int/disabilities/world_report/what_is_disability/en/

   First parenthetical citation (World Health Organization [WHO], 2012)

   Subsequent citations (WHO, 2012)

8o An Audio Podcast

To cite an audio podcast, provide the information required for regular radio broadcasts, recordings, or speeches (7d, 7e, or 7g). End the entry with the source and the URL.

Chang, A. (Host). (2020, January 24). *How public health officials use "contact tracing" to track an epidemic's spread* [Audio podcast]. NPR. https://www.npr.org/2020/01/24/799358631/how-public-health-officials-use-contact-tracing-to-track-an-epidemics-spread

   Parenthetical citation (Chang, 2020)

Kastenbaum, S. (Host). (2013, February 20). *NYC and the violently mentally ill* [Audio podcast]. CNN Radio. https://cnn.com/videos/us/2013/02/20/exp-kastenbaummentalill.cnn-radio

   Parenthetical citation (Kastenbaum, 2013)

8p A Posting—Blog, Discussion Group, Facebook, or Twitter

To cite a posting to a blog, discussion group, Facebook page, or Twitter account, provide the author, identified by name or screen name; the date of the posting; and the title of the posting in italics (or up to the first twenty words of the post), with a description of the message. Then identify the media platform, capitalized but without italics, followed by a period and the URL (without a closing period).

Ahmed, S. (2019, November 17). *5 types of people to "unfriend" on social media* [Facebook post]. CNN. https://cnn.com/2019/11/17/us/national-facebook-unfriend-day-trnd/index.html

   Parenthetical citation (Ahmed, 2019)

Burroughs, W. (2020, January 25). *The art of decision-making* [Tweet]. Twitter. https://twitter.com/WillBurroughs/status/1221090862551138304

   Parenthetical citation (Burroughs, 2020)

9 Examining Sample Papers

BEYOND BIRTH ORDER   1

**Beyond Birth Order:
Recognizing Other Variables**

Elissa Allen
Indiana State University

BEYOND BIRTH ORDER   2

Abstract

Although scholars continue to make a case for birth-order effects in children's development, exclusive reliance on this useful but one-dimensional criterion ignores other variables that affect children's personal, intellectual, and social development. The sex of other siblings, the time between births, the size of the family, the age of the mother, the psychological condition of the children, the absence of a parent, and the birth order of the parents also influence a child's development.

*Sidebar notes:*

A sample of student formatting appears on page 126

Running head: all capitals (38)

Identifying information: centered (27–28)

If an author note is required, it appears at the bottom of the title page (28).

Centered label, in boldface type, with normal capitalization (29)

Unindented that summarizes the paper's key ideas (29)

BEYOND BIRTH ORDER 3

**Beyond Birth Order:
Recognizing Other Variables**

Sigmund Freud, Queen Elizabeth II, Albert Einstein, William Shakespeare, George Washington, Jacqueline Kennedy, John Milton, Julius Caesar, Leontyne Price, and Winston Churchill. What do these famous people have in common? They were all first-born children. The fact that so many important people in all spheres of influence have been first-born children lends credence to the notion that birth order helps determine the kind of people we become.

Scientific studies over the years have, in fact, suggested that birth order affects an individual's development. For example, Pine (1995) suggested that first-born children acquire language skills sooner than later-born children. Skinner and Fox-Francoeur (2010) observed that first-born children use established procedures to solve problems, whereas later-born children use less predictable strategies. Kluger (2007) noted that later-born children are more inclined toward risky activities than are first-born children, and Sulloway (1995) observed that later-born children are more rebellious than first-born children. Further, Ernst and Angst (1983) explained the underlying premise of birth-order effects this way: "Everybody agrees that birth-order differences must arise from differential socialization by the parents. There is, however, no general theory on how this differential socialization actually works" (p. x). Yet other studies (Eckstein & Kaufman, 2012; Herrera et al., 2003; Salmon et al., 2012) suggested that parents' beliefs about birth-order differences influence their expectations for their children. Stein (2008) also observed that birth-order effects are more pronounced in families that are competitive and democratic, and Carette et al. (2011) noted that birth order establishes varied levels of emphasis on goal setting (first born) and on winning (last born). It is not surprising, then, that a general theory has not emerged because many other variables besides birth order influence an individual's personal, intellectual, and social development.

Sex of the Siblings

While acknowledging that birth order plays a part in an individual's development, scholars have begun to recognize that it is only one variable. For example, Sutton-Smith and Rosenberg (1970) observed that even in two-child families there are four possible variations for sibling relationships based on gender: (a) first-born female, second-born female; (b) first-born female, second-born male; (c) first-born male, second-born male; (d) first-born male, second-born female. In families with three children, the variations increase to 24. To suggest that being the first-born child is the same in all of these contexts ignores too many variables.

Time Between Births

Forer (1976) suggested that when the births of children are separated by 5 or more years, the effects of birth order are changed. For example, in a

BEYOND BIRTH ORDER

family with four children (with children aged 12, 6, 4, and 2 years old), the second child would be more likely to exhibit the characteristics of an oldest child because of the child's nearness in age to the younger children and the 6-year separation in age from the oldest child. The pattern would differ from that of a sibling in a four-child family if the children were spaced fewer than 3 years apart (for example, if the children were 10, 8, 5, and 3 years old); this second child would exhibit the characteristics typical of a second–middle child.

Comparative numbers in the same form (52)

Elissa's own example: no documentation required

Size of Family

Studies have also suggested that the size of the family modifies the effects of birth order (Kanazawa, 2012; Kristensen & Bjerkedal, 2007). In a moderate-sized family (two to four children), the first-born child usually achieves the highest level of education; however, Forer (1969) observed that "a first-born child from a large family has often been found to obtain less education than a last-born child from such a family" (p. 24). Whether this occurs because large families tend to have lower socioeconomic status or whether it is the result of varied family dynamics, the overall size of the family seems to alter the preconceived notions of birth order and its influence on a child's development (Hartshorne, 2010).

Age of the Mother

Studies have suggested that a mother's age has a strong bearing on the child's learned behavior, regardless of birth order (Bonesrønning & Massih,

2011; Booth & Kee, 2009). Sutton-Smith and Rosenberg (1970) offered this perspective:

> On a more obvious level, younger mothers have more stamina and vigor than older mothers. One speculation in the literature is that they are also more anxious and uncertain about their child-training procedures, and that this has an effect of inducing anxiety in their offspring. (p. 138)

It seems safe to assume, then, that the third child of a woman of 28 will have a different experience growing up than the third child of a woman of 39. They may share the same relational patterns with their siblings, but they will not share the same patterns with their mothers.

Psychological Factors

Early studies on birth order failed to account for psychological differences among children, even among those who shared the same birth status. Forer (1969) asserted, however, that "special conditions involving a child in a family may change the birth-order effect both for him and his siblings" (p. 19). Conditions such as a child's mental retardation, severe hearing loss, blindness, physical disabilities—or even exceptional beauty, intelligence, or physical skill—can alter the dynamics of the family and consequently affect the traditionally described effects of birth order (Forer, 1969, p. 19). In short, a middle child whose physiological conditions are outside the normal spectrum—because of different potential and opportunity—will not have the same life experiences as a middle child who is considered average.

BEYOND BIRTH ORDER

Absence of a Parent

Parents may be absent from family units for a variety of reasons: A parent may die, creating a permanent void in a family unit; a parent may be gone to war or be hospitalized for an extended period, creating a temporary but still notable disruption in the family; or a parent may travel for business, creating an irregular but obvious interruption in the family's normal workings. The loss of a parent can affect a child's experiences and can, under certain circumstances, mitigate the effects of birth order (Sulloway, 1997). Toman (1993) explained that the effects of parental absence will be greater

    a. The more recently they have occurred,
    b. The earlier in a person's life they have occurred,
    c. The older the person lost is (in relation to the oldest family member),
    d. The longer the person has lived together with the lost person,
    e. The smaller the family,
    f. The greater the imbalance of the sexes in the family resulting from the loss,
    g. The longer it takes the family to find a replacement for the lost person,
    h. The greater the number of losses, and the graver the losses, that have occurred before. (pp. 41–42)

Such disruptions—whether major or minor—alter the family unit and often have a greater influence on the children than the traditional effects of birth order.

BEYOND BIRTH ORDER 8

Birth Order of Parents

A number of scholars have asserted that the birth order of parents influences to a high degree their interrelationships with their children and, consequently, creates an impact that extends beyond the simple birth order of the children. Toman (1993) described the family relationships, based on birth order, that promise the least conflict and, consequently, the best situation for children's development:

> If the mother is the youngest sister of a brother and has an older son and a younger daughter, she can identify with her daughter and the daughter with the mother. The daughter, too, is the younger sister of a brother. Moreover, the mother has no trouble dealing with her son, for she had an older brother in her original family and her son, too, is an older brother of a sister. (p. 199)

A long quotation (75–76)

Toman's assumption that parents relate better to their children when they have shared similar sibling-related experiences leads to this assumption: When parents can create a positive and productive home environment (because of familiar familial relationships), the children will benefit. When conflict occurs because sibling relations are unfamiliar, everyone suffers. Parent–child relationships—determined, at least in part, by the parents' own birth orders—would consequently vary from family to family, even when children of those families share the same birth order.

BEYOND BIRTH ORDER

Conclusion

According to U.S. Census information collected from 92,119 randomly selected mothers, 28% of children are first born, 28% second born, 20% middle born, and 18% youngest born (as cited in Simpson et al., 1994). As long as census takers, scholars, family members, parents, and children think in terms of birth order, we will have an oversimplified perspective of why children develop as they do. Yet studies (Parish, 1990) have suggested that adolescents recognize that family structure and personal interaction have a stronger bearing on their perceptions of themselves, other family members, and their families than does either birth order or even gender. And, importantly, websites such as the Proceedings of the National Academy of Science (2020) approach the issue from varied—and often contradictory—perspectives through over 2,000 archived articles (https://www.pnas.org). Perhaps we should take our cues from these young people and current scholars and recognize that birth order is but one interesting variable in personality development.

BEYOND BIRTH ORDER 10

References

Bonesrønning, H., & Massih, S. S. (2011). Birth order effects on young students' academic achievement. *Journal of Socio-Economics, 40*(6), 824–832. https://doi.org/10.1016/j.socec.2011.08.010

Booth, A. L., & Kee, H. J. (2009). Birth order matters: The effect of family size and birth order on educational attainment. *Journal of Population Economics, 22,* 367–397. https://doi.org/10.1007/s00148-007-0181-4

Carette, B., Anseel, F., & Van Yperen, N. W. (2011). Born to learn or born to win? Birth order effects on achievement goals. *Journal of Research on Personality, 45*(5), 500–503. https://doi.org/10.1016/j.jrp.2011.06.008

Eckstein, D., & Kaufman, J. A. (2012). The role of birth order in personality: An enduring intellectual legacy of Alfred Adler. *Journal of Individual Psychology, 68*(1), 60–75.

Ernst, C., & Angst, J. (1983). *Birth order: Its influence on personality*. Springer.

Forer, L. K. (1969). *Birth order and life roles*. Thomas.

Forer, L. K. (1976). *The birth order factor: How your personality is influenced by your place in the family*. McKay.

Hartshorne, J. K. (2010). Ruled by birth order? *Scientific American Mind, 20*(7), 18–19. https://doi.org/10.1038/scientificamericanmind0100-18

Herrera, N. C., Zajonc, R. B., Wieczorkowska, G., & Cichomski, B. (2003). Beliefs about birth rank and their reflection in reality. *Journal of Personality and Social Psychology, 85*(1), 142–150. https://doi.org/10.1037/0022-3514.85.1.142

Kanazawa, S. (2012). Intelligence, birth order, and family size. *Personality and Social Psychology Bulletin, 38*(9), 1157–1164. https://doi.org/10.1177.0146167212445911

Kluger, J. (2007, October 29). The power of birth order. *Time, 170*(18), 42–48. http://content.time.com/time/magazine/article/0,9171,1673284,00.html

Kristensen, P., & Bjerkedal, T. (2007, 22 June). Explaining the relation between birth order and intelligence. *Science, 316*(5832), 1717. https://doi.org/10.1126/science.1141493

Parish, T. S. (1990). Evaluations of family by youth: Do they vary as a function of family structure, gender, and birth order? *Adolescence, 25*(98), 353–356.

Pine, J. M. (1995). Variations in vocabulary development as a function of birth order. *Child Development, 66*(1), 272–281. https://doi.org/10.111/j/1467-8624.1995.tb00870.x

Salmon, C. A., Shackelford, T. K., & Michalski, R. L. (2012). Birth order, sex of child, and perceptions of parental favoritism. *Personality and Individual Differences, 52*(3), 357–362. https://doi.org/10.1016/j.paid.2011.10.033

Simpson, P. W., Bloom, J. W., Newlon, B. J., & Arminio, L. (1994). Birth-order proportions of the general population in the United States. *Individual Psychology: Journal of Adlerian Theory, 50*(2), 173–182.

Skinner, N. F., & Fox-Francoeur, C. A. (2010). Personality implications of adaption–innovation: Birth order as a determinant of cognitive style. *Social Behavior and Personality, 38*(2), 237–240. https://doi.org/10.2224/sbp.2010.38.2.237

Stein, H. T. (2008). *Adlerian overview of birth order characteristics*. Alfred Adler Institutes of San Francisco. http://ourworld.compuserve.com/homepages/hstein/birthord.htm

Sulloway, F. J. (1995). Birth order and evolutionary psychology: A meta-analytic overview. *Psychological Inquiry, 6*(1), 75–80. https://doi.org/10.1207/s15327965pli0601-15

Sulloway, F. J. (1997). *Born to rebel: Birth order, family dynamics, and creative lives*. Vintage Books.

Sutton-Smith, B., & Rosenberg, B. G. (1970). *The sibling*. Holt.

Toman, W. (1993). *Family constellation: Its effects on personality and social behavior*. Springer.

> Article and webpage titles are italicized, but website titles are not (109).

SAMPLE WITH STUDENT FORMATTING

Only the page number is required (38).

The bold title is centered (28).

Course information is provided (28).

No author note is required (28).

1

**Beyond Birth Order:
Recognizing Other Variables**

Elissa Allen

Department of Psychology, Indiana State University

PSYCH 376: Psychological Research and Writing

Dr. Trina Estherman

April 10, 2020

No abstract is required; the text begins on page 2.

The content of the paper remains the same.

2

**Beyond Birth Order:
Recognizing Other Variables**

Sigmund Freud, Queen Elizabeth II, Albert Einstein, William Shakespeare, George Washington, Jacqueline Kennedy, John Milton, Julius Caesar, Leontyne Price, and Winston Churchill. What do these famous people have in common? They were all first-born children. The fact that so many important people in all spheres of influence have been first-born children lends credence to the notion that birth order helps determine the kind of people we become.

STUDENTS' REACTIONS   1

**Students' Reactions to Kinds of Test Questions:
A Piece of the Test-Anxiety Puzzle**

Gabriel Stevenson
Indiana State University

STUDENTS' REACTIONS   2

Abstract

The purpose of this brief study was to determine whether specific kinds of test questions produced anxiety in students. The results of a survey of 89 high school ninth graders indicate that true/false, multiple-choice, and matching are low-anxiety question formats, whereas essay, fill-in-the-blank, and listing are high-anxiety question formats. However, the study revealed that students' anxiety levels related to question types do not vary dramatically, either by question type or by students' performance levels, as indicated by previous grades.

Keywords: academic performance, questioning strategies, test anxiety.

STUDENTS' REACTIONS   3

**Students' Reactions to Kinds of Test Questions:
A Piece in the Test-Anxiety Puzzle**

Today's students are faced with an increasing number of tests. Not only do they take tests for their individual classes, but they also take state-mandated competency tests to progress through school and standardized achievement tests to gain admission to colleges and universities. With the emphasis currently being placed on tests, it is no wonder that many students are now experiencing test anxiety.

One area, however, has not received sufficient attention: students' reactions to specific kinds of test questions. Consequently, using data collected from a sampling of high school students, this brief study attempts to discover with what types of test questions students are most comfortable and what kinds of questioning techniques produce the greatest amount of insecurity or anxiety.

The nature of students' test anxiety has been—and continues to be—studied by scholars in education, psychology, and related fields. By understanding the forms, causes, and results of test anxiety, they hope to provide the means for students and educators to address the problem in helpful ways.

Scholars have noted that shifting cultural contexts—which require the regular use of competency tests—have contributed to increased test anxiety among students (Embse & Hasson, 2012; Spielberger & Vagg, 1995). Other scholars have described the nature of test anxiety,

STUDENTS' REACTIONS 4

providing useful categories and explanations to enhance the understanding of this multifaceted problem (Bower, 2011; Eum & Rice, 2011; Wigfield & Eccles, 1989). Others have contextualized the testing situation by describing the high-stakes educational environments in which tests are given (Cizek & Burg, 2006; Hancock, 2001).

Scholars have also explored the cognitive processes that are related to test anxiety. Schutz et al. (2002) have distinguished between high and low levels of test anxiety and have discussed the ways students perceive the test-taking process and the ways they cope. Others have addressed students' self-awareness about the emotional nature of the testing process and their own procedures for handling emotion during testing (Weiner, 1994; Zeidner, 1995a, 1995b, 2007). Birenbaum (2007) has extended discussions of test anxiety to incorporate students' instructional preferences and learning strategies.

Yet other scholars have discussed test anxiety among special student populations, noting that test anxiety among students with disabilities can lead to poor test performance, lead to poor overall academic performance, and create low self-esteem (Sena et al., 2007; Swanson & Howell, 1996). Further, Nelson et al. (2000) have presented information on alternatives to and adaptations of traditional testing that can allow special-needs students to demonstrate what they know without the additional burden of test anxiety.

Multiple references, separated by semicolons (73)

STUDENTS' REACTIONS 5

These studies have laid a contextual groundwork for further study. In particular, Salend (2011, 2012) has addressed practical issues of test design, such as organization, formatting, and length. However, no studies have addressed whether question types contribute directly to test anxiety. This brief, survey-based study may advance this work in a small but important way.

Method

Participants

The survey group was composed of 89 ninth-grade students (44 females and 45 males) from three classes. The students were enrolled in a required (and untracked) ninth-grade English class that included students of varied abilities at a consolidated high school in west-central Indiana. The students had completed one grading period; their grades from the previous term ranged from *A* to *F*.

Materials

Students were given a brief questionnaire (see Appendix) that included these elements: (a) an element to determine gender, (b) an element to record their grades in English during the previous 9 weeks, and (c) a six-element questionnaire using a Likert-type scale so that students could indicate their anxiety-related responses to six types of test questions.

Procedures

The students' teacher distributed the questionnaire at the beginning of each of the three class periods and read the instructions aloud, emphasizing that students should respond to the types of questions

STUDENTS' REACTIONS 6

based on their entire testing experiences, not just those on English tests. Students were then given 10 minutes to complete the questionnaire; most completed the questionnaires in fewer than 5 minutes.

Results

The most general analysis of the data involved computing students' ratings of question types using the Likert-type scale (1–2 = *secure*, 3–4 = *no reaction*, 5–6 = *insecure*). Percentages of students' responses appear in Table 1.

Low-Anxiety Question Types

The findings indicated that true/false test questions created the least anxiety, with 31.4% of students giving them a 1 rating; in addition, 81.9% rated true/false as a 1, 2, or 3, indicating little anxiety. Matching and multiple-choice questions also achieved low anxiety ratings, with 25.8% of students giving them a 1 rating; 79.7% rated matching as a 1, 2, or 3, indicating little anxiety. Interestingly, 84.3% rated multiple-choice questions as a 1, 2, or 3, making multiple choice the question type that produces the least anxiety in the greatest percentage of students.

High-Anxiety Question Types

The findings indicated that essay questions created the most anxiety, with 49.4% of students giving them a 6 rating; further, 71.9% rated essay questions as a 4, 5, or 6, indicating a high degree of anxiety. Fill-in-the-blank questions also achieved a high-anxiety rating, with 24.6% of students giving them a 6 rating; 65.1% rated fill-in-the-blank questions as a 4, 5, or 6, indicating a high degree of anxiety. Finally, 21.4% of students rated listing questions as a 6; 65.3% rated them as a 4, 5, or 6, making this a high-stress question type.

Mean Responses

The mean responses to the question types (1–2 = *secure*, 3–4 = *no reaction*, 5–6 = *insecure*) correlated with the individual low-anxiety and high-anxiety ratings given by students, as shown in Figure 1. True/false (2.35), multiple-choice (2.43), and matching (2.53) remained in the low-anxiety category, but multiple-choice and matching reversed their rating order. Essay (4.56), fill- in-the-blank (4.27), and listing (4.16) remained in the high-anxiety category; they retained the same rating order.

As Figure 1 illustrates, mean responses by students' grade categories showed slightly varied preferences among high-performing and low-performing students: *A* students (1: matching; 2: multiple-choice; 3: true/false; 4: fill-in-the-blank; 5–6: listing and essay), *B* students (1: multiple-choice; 2: matching; 3: true/false; 4: listing; 5–6: fill-in-the-blank and essay), *C* students (1: matching; 2: multiple-choice; 3: true/false; 4–5: fill-in-the-blank and listing; 6: essay), *D* students (1: true/false; 2: multiple-choice; 3: matching; 4: listing; 5: fill-in-the-blank; 6: essay), and *F* students (1: true/false; 2: multiple-choice; 3: matching; 4: listing; 5: fill-in-the-blank; 6: essay).

An average of the mean responses to all six question types for each grade category indicated an increasing degree of anxiety: for *A* students, the averaged mean response was 2.75; for *B* students,

3.08; for *C* students, 3.57; for *D* students, 3.61; and for *F* students, 3.83. Although the increments were small, there was a steady progression from one student group to the next; however, none of the averaged means fell far from the 3–4 range (*no reaction*), suggesting that, generally, no question format made students as a group feel either very secure or very anxious.

Discussion

The data indicate that, for students, question types fall into two distinct groups: low-stress questions (true/false, multiple-choice, matching) and high-stress questions (listing, fill-in-the-blank, essay). However, the data also indicate that, on average, students' anxiety levels related to question types do not vary greatly (mean responses ranged from 2.75 for *A* students to 3.83 for *F* students), which suggests that although question-related anxiety exists, it is not dramatic.

An analysis of the data further indicates that low-anxiety questions (true/false, multiple-choice, matching) are format-based, providing information and allowing students to select among options.

In contrast, high-anxiety questions (listing, fill-in-the-blank, essay) are open-ended, requiring students to recall and arrange information on their own.

The results of this brief study are, of course, tentative and need to be reproduced with a larger, more comprehensive sample. However, the study does suggest the value of analyzing specific question formats because they can contribute in a small but significant way to overall test anxiety.

"Discussion" section: comments on the data, correlates with the hypothesis (31)

A comment on the value of the study (31)

References

Birenbaum, M. (2007). Assessment and instruction preferences and their relationship with test anxiety and learning strategies. *Higher Education, 53*(6), 749–768. https://doi.org/10.1007/s10734-005-4843-4

Bower, B. (2011). The write stuff for test anxiety. *Science News, 179*(4), 9.

Cizek, J. C., & Burg, S. S. (2006). *Addressing test anxiety in a high-stakes environment.* Corwin Press.

Embse, N., & Hasson, R. (2012). Test anxiety and high-stakes test performance between school settings: Implications for education. *Preventing School Failure, 56*(3), 180–187. https://doi.org/10.1080/1045988x.2011.633285

Eum, K. U., & Rice, K. G. (2011). Test anxiety, perfectionism, goal orientation, and academic performance. *Anxiety, Stress, and Coping, 24*(2), 167–178. https://doi.org/10.1080/10615806.2010.488723

Hancock, D. R. (2001). Effects of test anxiety and evaluative threat on students' achievement and motivation. *The Journal of Educational Research, 94*(5), 284–290. https://doi.org/10.1080/00220670109598764

Nelson, J. S., Jayanthi, M., Epstein, M. H., & Bursuck, W. D. (2000). Student preferences for adaptations in classroom testing. *Remedial and Special Education, 21*(1), 41–52. https://doi.org/10.1177/074193250002100106

Salend, S. J. (2011). Addressing test anxiety. *Teaching Exceptional Children, 44*(2), 58–68. https://doi.org/10.1177/004005991104400206

Salend, S. J. (2012). Teaching students not to sweat the test: Teachers can change some of their practices to ensure that students don't feel extreme anxiety at exam time. *Phi Delta Kappan, 93*(6), 20–25. https://doi.org/10.1177/003172171209300605

Schutz, P. A., Davis, H. A., & Schwanenflugel, P. J. (2002). Organization of concepts relevant to emotions and their regulation during test taking. *The Journal of Experimental Education, 70*(4), 316–342. https://doi.org/10.1080/00220970209599511

Sena, J. D. W., Lowe, P. A., & Lee, S. W. (2007). Significant predictors of test anxiety among students with and without learning disabilities. *Journal of Learning Disabilities, 40*(4), 370–376. https://doi.org/10.1177/00222194070400040601

Spielberger, C. D., & Vagg, P. R. (Eds.). (1995). *Test anxiety: Theory, assessment, and treatment*. Taylor.

Swanson, S., & Howell, C. (1996). Test anxiety in adolescents with learning disabilities and behavior disorders. *Exceptional Children, 62*(5), 389–397. https://doi.org/10.1177/001440299606200501

Weiner, B. (1994). Integrating social and personal theories of achievement striving. *Review of Educational Research, 64*(4), 557–573. https://doi.org/10.3102/00346543064004557

STUDENTS' REACTIONS 10

Wigfield, A., & Eccles, J. S. (1989). Test anxiety in elementary and secondary school students. *Educational Psychologist, 24*(2), 159–183. https://doi.org/10.1207/s15326985ep2402_3

Zeidner, M. (1995a). Adaptive coping with test situations: A review of the literature. *Educational Psychologist, 30*(3), 123–133. https://doi.org/10.1207/s15326985ep3003_3

Zeidner, M. (1995b). Coping with examination stress: Resources, strategies, outcomes. *Anxiety, Stress, and Coping, 8*(4), 279–298. https://doi.org/10.1080/10615809508249379

Zeidner, M. (2007). Test anxiety in educational contexts: Concepts, findings, and future directions. In P. A. Schutz & R. Pekrun (Eds.), *Emotion in education* (pp. 165–184). Academic Press. https://doi.org/10.1016/b978-012372545-5/50011-3

Names repeated in subsequent entries (70)

STUDENTS' REACTIONS

Table 1

Overall Responses (Security to Insecurity) to Question Types

			Rating			
Question type	1	2	3	4	5	6
Matching	25.8	30.3	23.6	11.2	3.4	5.6
True/false	31.4	25.8	24.7	13.5	3.4	1.1
Fill-in-the-blank	2.2	10.1	22.5	13.5	27.0	24.6
Multiple-choice	25.8	32.6	25.9	6.7	6.7	2.2
Listing	4.5	5.6	24.7	21.4	22.5	21.4
Essay	6.8	13.5	7.9	10.1	12.4	49.4

- Sequential page numbers (33)
- Numbered table, in boldface type, on a separate page (33)
- Table title in italics (33)
- Ruled lines to separate elements (33)
- Column spacing adjusted for easy reading (33).

STUDENTS' REACTIONS

Figure 1

Mean Responses to Questions by Student Grade Categories

— A students
--- B students
······· C students
— D students
--- F students

- Numbered figure on a separate page (34)

STUDENTS' REACTIONS

Appendix

Test Anxiety Questionnaire

Survey: Test Anxiety—Reactions to Kinds of Test Questions

M   F

Grade Last 9 Weeks: A   B   C   D   F

Circle one response for each kind of test question: *1* means that you feel *comfortable/secure* with these kinds of questions (you won't worry about that part of the test); *6* means that you feel *uncomfortable/insecure* with these question types (you will worry about how you do on that part of the test). Consider tests for all classes, not just English.

		Secure		No reaction		Insecure	
1.	Matching	1	2	3	4	5	6
2.	True/false	1	2	3	4	5	6
3.	Fill-in-the-blank	1	2	3	4	5	6
4.	Multiple-choice	1	2	3	4	5	6
5.	Listing	1	2	3	4	5	6
6.	Essay	1	2	3	4	5	6

A Preparing an Annotated Bibliography

Objectives:

- Learn to prepare an annotated bibliography following formatting guidelines.
- Learn to create annotations that effectively evaluate potential sources.

The word *annotate* means to explain, to comment, or to evaluate. An annotated bibliography, as a result, is an alphabetical listing of sources for a paper or project with assessments of the sources; it contains a complete bibliographic entry for each source (providing the information required in a reference-list entry), followed by a brief paragraph or multiple paragraphs that analyze the source. Annotated bibliographies are often created as part of the research process—at a stage between completing research and writing the paper or planning the presentation.

A1 Following Format Guidelines

Because an annotated bibliography is usually presented as a separate assignment (rather than substituted for a traditional reference section in a paper), the guidelines included here are for a separate assignment.

Applying General Guidelines

Prepare a standard title page, noting that only the title follows a distinct pattern. For the title, include your research topic (not the potential title for your paper), followed by a colon and the phrase *Annotated Bibliography* (not italicized); use boldface type (for example: **Birth Order: Annotated Bibliography**). Then include your name, affiliation, course information, instructor name, and the due date; in other words, follow regular guidelines for the title page.

On the second page, three spaces below the page number, type the descriptive title (in boldface type); two lines below, begin the annotated bibliography, keeping these familiar guidelines in mind:

- Double-space throughout.
- Alphabetize your bibliographic entries (as you would reference-list entries).

- Provide complete bibliographic entries (which include the same information as traditional reference-list entries), following the guidelines in Chapters 4–8.
- Indent second and subsequent lines of entries, as always.

Positioning Your Annotations

Each annotation is a new paragraph, beginning two lines below the bibliographic entry; it is indented five spaces (like a long quotation). If an annotation contains multiple paragraphs, the first lines of subsequent paragraphs are indented an additional five spaces.

A2 Thinking About the Content of Annotations

Annotations are typically 100–200 words; however, they may be briefer or longer if the context requires brevity or elaboration. Similarly, the content of an annotation can vary considerably, depending on the writing context and the kinds of sources being evaluated. When an annotated bibliography is assigned, follow your instructor's guidance about length and focus.

Although you will never be expected to address all of these topics, approach writing annotations by considering these potential areas of focus, which are as varied as potential sources:

- **Description.** Explain the source's basic features (a 16-page article in a professional journal; a one-page editorial in a national newspaper; a 12-chapter book from a university press).
- **Author or authors.** Identify the author or authors and comment on their expertise or affiliations (author of numerous articles and books; affiliated with a national foundation; no known scholarly publications).
- **Perspective.** Consider the approach to the topic (broad overview of the subject; narrow focus on a subtopic; intended for fellow professionals; intended for a general audience).
- **Scholarly approach.** Explain the way in which the work is developed (based on primary research; summary of existing data; based on personal experience or anecdotes).
- **Evaluation.** Consider the strengths and shortcomings of the source (clear writing; excellent tables and charts; weak organization; dated information).
- **Potential value for your paper.** Discuss whether the source or some parts of it will be useful for your research (helpful

introduction; very well written and therefore quotable; too narrowly focused; limited sample size).

- **Relevance.** Comment of whether the source approaches the topic in a way that is suited to your research (the topic is clear, but the approach is business-oriented).
- **Currency.** Explain how the currency of a source's information will suit your needs (current data; dated assumptions about gender roles; contemporary reinterpretations of older data; historically important perspective).
- **Comparison.** Comment on how a source compares with other sources (suitable information but repeats what is found in multiple sources; the best use of graphics in any source).
- **Style.** Discuss how the author's style enhances or detracts from the source (jargon-free sentences make ideas especially clear; overly long sentences make this source almost unreadable).

A3 Planning Annotations

After reviewing the alternatives that can be used to assess a source, decide which topics provide the best way to assess the source. Although a shared focus should unify your annotations (all, for example, might include a description of the source, a comment on the author's credentials, and a discussion of the source's scholarly approach), distinguish among your varied sources by also addressing topics that are appropriate to each source.

Remember as well that your instructor may ask for a uniform approach to your annotations, in which case you should follow the assignment guidelines and address the topics that are identified for you.

A4 Creating the Elements of an Annotated Bibliography

Some writers begin by creating full bibliographic entries for all sources and then creating the annotations at a subsequent stage. Others prefer to create the first bibliographic entry and its annotation and then move to the second entry and annotation, continuing this process until the work is done. Choose whichever pattern is best matched to your writing process.

After you select the topics to cover, decide on the order in which to present them. Then begin writing—being aware that an annotation may require multiple revisions in order to present ideas clearly and compactly. If an annotation is too brief, add additional details; if it is too long, either work to eliminate extraneous words and phrases or eliminate some details.

Writing critically and concisely takes practice, so allow sufficient time to plan, write, revise, and develop the final annotated bibliography. Through careful work, you will demonstrate to your instructor (or other readers) that you have read (or viewed or listened to) your sources, that you have reviewed them critically, and that you have shared your informed judgments with care.

Sample Annotation—Fully Developed

Birth Order: Annotated Bibliography

Toman, W. (1993). *Family constellation: Its effects on personality and social behavior*. Springer. This 16-chapter book, in its fourth edition, provides a general overview of birth-order theory. Its author, Walter Toman, is an Austrian-born psychologist who taught at Harvard University and Brandeis University and published numerous books on family relationships, as well as family counseling. The book presents a foundational discussion of birth order; the writing is clear, the examples are universal, and the discussions of variables that affect birth order are illuminating. With a 1993 publication, the book's specific data is undoubtedly dated; however, the clarity of its discussions of general principles of birth-order theory make it a worthwhile source—and its well-phrased sentences make it very quotable. It's very likely that I will use this source.

The descriptive title, in boldface type, appears first.

Full bibliographic entry

Description of the source; discussion of the author's credentials

General assessment; comment on currency

Observation on style; indication of potential value

Sample Annotated Bibliography With Student Formatting

Descriptive title

Birth Order: Annotated Bibliography

Other elements of the title page are the same as for other papers.

Elissa Allen

Department of Psychology, Indiana State University

PSYCH 376: Psychological Research and Writing

Dr. Trina Estherman

April 10, 2020

Birth Order: Annotated Bibliography

Kanazawa, S. (2012). Intelligence, birth order, and family size. *Personality and Social Psychology Bulletin, 39*(9), 1157–1164. https://doi.org/10.1177.01467212445911
  With data drawn from a national child-development study in the United Kingdom, this 8-page article asserts that birth order does not determine intelligence; rather, it claims that family size is the primary determiner of children's . . . .

Kluger, J. (2007, October 29). The power of birth order. *Time, 170*(18), 42–48. http://content.time.com/time/magazine/article/0,9171,1673284,00.html
  Written for a general audience, Kluger's 6-page cover story provides a useful overview of birth-order theory, bolstered by quotations and data from researchers from University of California—Berkeley, Stanford University, University of Texas, and other prestigious schools . . . .

Toman, W. (1993). *Family constellation: Its effects on personality and social behavior.* Springer.
  This 16-chapter book, in its fourth edition, provides a general overview of birth-order theory. Its author, Walter Toman, is an Austrian-born psychologist who taught at Harvard University and Brandeis University and published numerous books on family relationships, as well as . . . .

Descriptive title

Full bibliographic entry

Annotation, indented, begins on a new line.

(These annotations are shortened to show multiple samples.)

No extra space between sources and annotations

B. Preparing PowerPoint and Poster Presentations

Objectives:
- Learn to prepare a PowerPoint with suitable content, effective design, and balanced presentation.
- Learn to prepare a poster session that includes an effective display and a thoughtful presentation.

Presentations, essentially speeches supported by visual materials, provide unique opportunities. They allow you to share the results of either text-based or experimental research in visually oriented and interactive ways. Whether these presentations use a PowerPoint or poster format, the experience of preparing information in alternative ways develops helpful academic skills. In addition, presentations give you the chance to strengthen your ability to speak informatively to a group—an important professional skill.

B1 Preparing a PowerPoint Presentation

Originally designed for business applications, PowerPoint and other similar software allow writers to prepare slides to illustrate ideas for presentations. In an academic setting, PowerPoint presentations allow students to share ideas and information in visually interesting ways.

Thinking About a PowerPoint Presentation

With its capability to include a wide range of graphic images, PowerPoint software allows you to create visual support for presentations. However, as you think about preparing and delivering a PowerPoint presentation, it is essential to remember that you and your ideas and information should be the primary focus, not the images on the slides.

Planning for a PowerPoint Presentation

In some instances, your presentation may be based on work for another class project; for example, the PowerPoint may be a class presentation of your research findings from a paper or report. In that case, the preliminary work is complete, and you can concentrate on the structure, design, and delivery elements of the presentation. In other instances, the presentation may be a fully separate project. In that case, research to secure your content and then turn your attention to structure, design, and delivery. In either circumstance, allow yourself sufficient time to complete the preliminary work, to prepare your slides, and to practice the presentation itself.

Thinking About Content—General Considerations

To get an overall sense of how to prepare PowerPoint slides most effectively, think about your content in a holistic way. Consider these suggestions.

- **Think about your time allotment.** Consider the level of detail you can include based on your time limit. A 5-minute presentation can provide only the broadest overview, whereas a 15-minute presentation can include more detail.

- **Consider your audience's level of knowledge.** What is your audience likely to know about the topic of your presentation? Will you need to define terms? Will you need to explain research methodology? Or is your audience conversant with the topic, terminology, and methods? The more your audience knows, the more directly you can approach your presentation.

- **Think about organization and development.** All presentations need a beginning, middle, and end, but the best presentations follow clear, familiar organizational patterns for the middle section: chronological order (historical overviews, descriptions of processes), order of importance (explanations of subtopics, persuasive arguments), comparison–contrast (reviews of alternative ideas, explanations of opposing views), and others. Arrange the topics of your presentation judiciously and then provide information and images that develop each topic.

NOTE: If your presentation is based on a paper or report, you can follow that structure *or* develop an alternative plan.

Thinking About Content—Specific Considerations

After you have a general sense of how to focus your presentation, think about what specific content elements are needed for an effective presentation. Consider these recommendations.

- **Include a title slide.** Begin with a slide that includes the title of the presentation, your name, the course number and name, and the date. This slide functions like the title page of a paper or book and provides basic identifying information.
- **Consider including a preview slide.** As an option, include a slide that previews the main ideas of the presentation. Like a brief table of contents or a chapter preview, it lets your audience know the key points that you will address.
- **Present your information in a series of slides.** Prepare a series of slides that identifies the main points, provides explanations and samples, and incorporates images. It is easier to follow a presentation with a large number of slides (when each contains a small amount of information) than it is to follow a presentation with only a few slides that contain too much information. (See the section "Thinking About Graphic Design.")
- **Consider using a summary slide.** As an option, include a slide at the end of your presentation that reiterates its main points. A simple presentation probably doesn't need a summary slide, but a longer one probably does.
- **Include a reference-list slide.** To acknowledge your sources, include a slide that contains citations for the materials you have used; it functions like the reference page of a paper. Make sure that the information is complete and that it is appropriately formatted.
- **Prepare a speaking script.** Develop an outline of key points from which to speak. Include references to your slides so that you remember to change slides at the appropriate time. Do not merely read from the slides; rather, provide a separate commentary that includes more information than the slides themselves contain. Also, include transitions between sections of the presentation to emphasize the logical connections between the elements.

NOTE: Many people find it helpful to transfer the speaking script onto numbered note cards (4-by-6 or 5-by-7 inches) because cards are easier to handle than sheets of paper.

- **Consider preparing a handout.** To provide a clear and helpful record of your presentation, prepare a one- to two-page handout that summarizes the ideas of the presentation. A hand-out prepared in prose allows you to articulate ideas fully and include many of the details from your speaking script, as well as the slides.

NOTE: If you give audience members only the printed slides, then you have given them only the visual portion of your presentation, omitting your important commentary.

Thinking About Graphic Design

The design of the slides themselves is a key element of a PowerPoint presentation. You should create slides that are appropriate to your topic and consistent with your approach. Consider these strategies.

- **Let the content guide you.** *What* you choose to put on a slide should determine *how* you present the slide. To present a three-step sequence, use a numbered list. To present four alternatives, use a bulleted list (which does not imply a specific order). To compare data, use a simple table. In other words, let the content and purpose guide the design, not the other way around.
- **Strive for visual clarity.** Because your audience will be listening to you, as well as looking at your slides, do not overload slides with unnecessary information or graphics.
- **Make basic design choices that suit your content.** PowerPoint provides a number of slide templates: a band of color at the top, a band of color down the side, an ink-splatter, a row of colored cubes, and so on. Use these familiar styles with the understanding that people may have seen them before. Alternatively, you can go online to secure additional template styles or create a unique style yourself. Whichever pattern you choose, avoid visual clutter and suit the style to the content.

NOTE: Create balance with your slides. Leave visual space at the margins and between elements (known as "white space" on typed documents) and make sure that all of the slides contain approximately the same amount of information or graphics.

- **Choose color themes carefully.** Because colors create impressions and indicate mood, select color palettes that complement, rather than detract from, your presentation. Vibrant colors (vivid pink, sunny yellow, bright blue, acid green) work best for informal or lighthearted topics, whereas subdued colors (maroon, gold, navy blue, avocado) work best for formal or serious topics. Colors used in small amounts (sidebars, ruled lines, frames) can be bold without being overwhelming. However, when intense colors are used generously (background, print), they can become oppressive.

NOTE: If you choose color (rather than the standard black) for print features, make sure that it contrasts sufficiently with the background and can be easily read when projected.

Preparing a PowerPoint Presentation

- **Select fonts with care.** Choose font styles that are visually distinct when projected. Use large point sizes (24–36 is a reasonable range), so that audience members can read the text without difficulty. If you choose to vary fonts in your slides (for example, one font for titles and headings and a different font for primary text) or to vary point sizes (for example, 36 point for headings and 28 point for primary text), be sure to do so consistently.

NOTE: Avoid unusual decorative or display fonts. They project badly on some screens and can create an unprofessional impression.

- **Find images that enhance the presentation.** Include distinct visual elements that contribute to your presentation. Find images that are unique, make sure that they are of high quality, and reproduce their aspect ratio correctly. When possible, crop (cut down) the images to eliminate extraneous detail.

NOTE: Avoid familiar clip art images. Such works add nothing individual to your presentation. Instead, they are merely visual clichés, which can detract from your work.

- **Use charts, graphs, and tables when appropriate.** Use pie charts to show percentages, bar graphs to show comparisons, line graphs to show changes, and tables to show comparisons. Keep the designs simple and uncluttered, make the labels clear, and use color selectively for contrast.

- **Use numbered lists for sequential information.** When describing a process or a topic that must be addressed in a fixed order, use a numbered list. Use a small number per slide (generally 3–6) and make sure that the elements are presented in parallel form (words, phrases, or brief sentences).

- **Use bullet points to present alternatives.** Because bullet points signal elements that are nonsequential and roughly equivalent, they are especially helpful in a PowerPoint presentation. Use a small number on each slide (generally 3–6) and make sure that the elements are presented in parallel form (words, phrases, or brief sentences).

- **Use audio selectively.** Because audio is often difficult to adjust in a classroom or meeting space, use it selectively and always do a sound check before your presentation. Music can sometimes underscore a presentation, like the soundtrack of a film, and a spoken audio, if aptly chosen, can create interest.

But sound effects are often disruptive or even comical—neither of which enhances your presentation.

- **Incorporate video clips when they serve a specific purpose.** Incorporating video links within a PowerPoint presentation can create a dynamic change of pace. However, the video clip must be well-selected, brief, and directly related to the content of your presentation. Before the presentation, test the clip to ensure that the internet connection works.
- **Avoid visual clutter.** Keep the elements of each slide as uncluttered as possible. A few lines of text and some graphic elements are usually enough. While some people offer rigid guidelines (for example, no more than six lines and no more than six words per line), there are no "rules." However, the general principle of showing only a few elements at a time makes a great deal of sense.
- **Avoid "technical clutter."** PowerPoint provides a number of "animation" features: "cuts," "drop-in" elements, "fades," "reveals," "zooms," and others. While each feature can be interesting and purposeful, using too many suggests that technology, rather than content, is the focus of a presentation. Consequently, use animation features only if they serve content-related purposes. Otherwise, your audience will notice the technical "tricks," rather than the entire presentation.

Effective PowerPoint Slide
This slide uses color effectively, and the black print on a neutral background does not detract from the images.

Preparing a PowerPoint Presentation — B1 — 153

Ineffective PowerPoint Slide
This slide uses a title color that does not correspond with the images; further, the white print on a black background may be difficult to read.

Thinking About Technical Matters

Because PowerPoint slides provide a limited amount of information and selected visual images, they need to be carefully done. An error that might go unnoticed on a double-spaced page of text stands out dramatically in the spare (and enlarged) image projected on a screen. Give special attention to these procedures.

- **Proofread for errors.** Review your slides to ensure that you have consistently capitalized words in bulleted lists, punctuated parallel elements in parallel ways, and double-checked mechanical elements (spelling, italics, line spacing, and so on).
- **Proofread your citations.** If you include a reference list, provide complete information in correctly formatted citations.

Thinking About the Presentation

Because your comments will create the context for the PowerPoint slides, give serious attention to the "performance" elements of the presentation. Consider these strategies.

- **Analyze the room.** Think strategically about the presentation space. If the room is very large, modify the size of your images and adjust your speaking volume; if the room has windows without darkening shades, give special consideration to the clarity of your images; if the projection screen is small, then limit the amount of information on each slide. Also, think about sight lines; you want to ensure that audience members can see both you and your slides.

- **Think about the equipment.** The size of the screen and the quality of the projection equipment will affect how you design your presentation. The larger the screen and the better the equipment, the more flexibility you will have. Because a wireless remote allows you to control the projector from any location, use one if it is available.

NOTE: Do not assume, as many people do, that you can access your PowerPoint slides through an internet connection in the presentation space. While this usually is workable, connections aren't always available. To avoid potential delays, embarrassment, or other problems, always take your PowerPoint on a flash drive.

- **Consider what to wear.** You don't necessarily need to wear a suit or a dress, but select clothing that looks polished and that isn't distracting. How you look has a bearing on the professionalism of the presentation.

- **Rehearse your comments.** Practice using your speaking script. As you rehearse, you will discover effective phrasing and suitable ways to explain ideas; in addition, the practice will help you feel more secure about what you have to say and how to say it best. It will also allow you to adjust your comments to fit the time limit.

- **Think about your delivery.** When you make your presentation, face the audience as much as possible—not the projection screen. Make eye contact with audience members in all parts of the room. If space and technology allow, move around the front of the room; stepping away from a lectern or podium creates a more dynamic performance. Speak loudly enough that you can be heard throughout the room, pace yourself so that you don't seem rushed, and be enthusiastic. Most of all, don't stand at the podium and read the slides—without question, the dullest approach to a PowerPoint presentation.

- **Plan for questions.** Think critically and predict questions that your audience might pose; then practice responding to those questions.
- **Think about how to incorporate a handout.** If your presentation is substantive and you have prepared a handout, plan to distribute it *after* the presentation. Otherwise, your audience is likely to read through the handout, rather than listen to your presentation. As a courtesy, tell your audience in your introductory comments that you will share a handout after the presentation so that they won't spend time taking notes.

PowerPoint presentations provide a dynamic and visually oriented way to share the results of research. Their multidimensional approach—the blending of printed text, graphics, and oral presentation—makes them an effective means to share the results of your research work.

B2 Preparing a Poster Presentation

Poster presentations developed as part of professional meetings. Recognizing that traditional, speech-based sessions limited the scope of conferences, organizers searched for ways in which to involve a greater number of researchers in conference activities, as well as to provide opportunities for people to share preliminary findings or to solicit reactions to "work in progress." Because poster presentations are now a common way to share research, teachers have begun to incorporate the format into their classroom activities so that student researchers can develop skills in presenting their findings in interactive ways.

Thinking About a Poster Presentation

Poster presentations emphasize visual elements, supported with printed information, and allow researchers to discuss their work with interested people.

At conferences, presenters are allotted a predetermined amount of space (4-by-4 feet, 4-by-8 feet, or sometimes more) in an exhibit hall and display their posters for review for an allotted amount of time (1 hour or sometimes longer). Presenters stay with their posters, explain their work, answer questions, and solicit reactions. The visual presentation of research findings provides an exciting alternative to traditional speeches (which are often readings of papers), and the interactive format allows for more give-and-take among those who attend conferences.

In classes and seminars, poster presentations allow students to present their research to the entire class, as opposed to just the teacher, and to gather helpful reactions to their work.

Identifying the Features of a Poster Presentation

Whether given at a conference or in a classroom, poster presentations share a variety of features, which may be surprisingly simple or highly elaborate.

- **Display surface.** The simplest poster can be prepared on a standard 30-by-40-inch sheet of poster board, mounted for stability. Displayed on an easel for easy viewing, this kind of poster is most commonly presented in the classroom. More elaborate posters are prepared as freestanding displays, may include multiple display panels, and may be quite expensive to prepare. Such complex posters are more commonly presented at conferences.

- **Content.** To ensure that people focus properly on your work, create a clear and interesting title for the poster and provide your name and affiliation. Because posters of all kinds must present content in a concise, easily readable form, use headings judiciously. The standard divisions of a research paper—method, results, discussion, and others—provide familiar ways to divide the content of the poster, although other organizational patterns are also acceptable.

- **Visual elements.** Because posters emphasize the visual presentation of research findings, use graphic elements to your advantage. Arrange information for easy interpretation, remembering that readers scan visual documents in the same way they read: from left to right and from top to bottom. When possible, reduce material to bulleted lists for easy scanning. Select simple fonts in sizes that can be read from 3 to 6 feet away. Use tables, charts, graphs, and images to clarify ideas. Employ color, when possible, to create visual interest.

- **Supporting documents.** Provide a one- to two-page supporting document that summarizes the information presented on your poster. Label it clearly with the presentation's title and your identifying information; also include key elements from the poster. Make copies for those attending the conference or for class members.

- **Presentation.** You must facilitate the review of the poster. Without simply reading or summarizing the material for your audience (after all, they can do that), highlight key features and direct their attention to the most salient points. Also, be prepared to answer questions and guide discussion.

Planning for a Poster Presentation

Because poster presentations provide a unique opportunity to share research findings, a well-planned presentation takes time to prepare and requires unique kinds of effort. Consider these suggestions.

- **Allow yourself sufficient time.** Do not assume that a poster session is easy to prepare. Not only does it require initial research, but it also warrants specialized preparation that may be new to you if you are used to preparing only written documents. Also, because the presentation includes more kinds of elements—visual and speaking components, as well as written content—preparing the poster presentation should not be a rushed effort.
- **Experiment with design elements.** Explore alternative ways to design your poster. Prepare material in several formats (try different fonts and font sizes; use different color combinations; prepare tables *and* figures), and then decide which format creates the best visual effect.
- **Solicit reactions.** Seek responses to your work. Ask for overall reactions but also ask specific questions about presentational elements. If you have prepared alternative versions of your poster, ask which is most effective.
- **Practice your presentation.** Although a well-prepared poster should in some regards "speak for itself," consider the ways in which you can help an audience review your poster. Develop a set of "talking points," a brief list of comments to guide your explanations. Practice your presentation to ensure that your expression is clear and helpful.
- **Anticipate questions.** Think critically and predict questions that your audience might pose; then practice responding to those questions.

Poster presentations provide a unique way to share the results of research. Their conciseness, visual clarity, and interactivity make them an effective means of sharing the results of your research work.

Students' Reactions to Kinds of Test Questions: A Piece of the Test-Anxiety Puzzle

Gabriel Stevenson
CIMT 451

Student Research Day
April 20, 2020

Student Programs
Hulman Memorial
Student Union

Participants
- 89 high school students
- 44 female students
- 45 male students
- enrolled in 9th-grade English class
- consolidated school in west-central Indiana

Materials: Brief Questionnaire
- identify gender
- English grade the previous 9 weeks
- 6-element questionnaire about question types (matching, true–false, fill-in-the-blank, multiple choice, listing, essay); 6-point Likert-type scale

Procedure:
- read the instructions aloud
- emphasize complete school experience
- allotted 10 minutes to complete the questionnaire
- most completed the questionnaire in fewer than 5 minutes

	SECURE		NO REACTION		INSECURE	
Question Type	1	2	3	4	5	6
Matching	25.8	30.3	23.6	11.2	3.4	5.6
True/false	31.4	25.8	24.7	13.5	3.4	1.1
Fill-in-the-blank	2.2	10.1	22.5	13.5	27.0	24.6
Multiple-choice	25.8	32.6	26.9	6.7	6.7	2.2
Listing	4.5	5.6	24.7	21.4	22.5	21.4
Essay	6.8	13.5	7.9	10.1	12.4	49.4

Robert Perrin

Sample Poster

C Addressing Technical Issues in Writing

Objectives:

- Learn to recognize the most common technical problems that interfere with effective writing.
- Learn alternative strategies to avoid these common problems.
- Learn techniques for creating informal and formal outlines.

Common Technical Problems

C1 Fragments
C2 Comma Splices and Fused Sentences
C3 Pronoun Reference
C4 Pronoun Case
C5 Positioning Modifiers
C6 Active and Passive Voice
C7 Possessives and Contractions
C8 Outlining

C1 Fragments

Fragments are capitalized and punctuated as if they were sentences, but instead, they are either subordinate clauses or phrases lacking subjects or verbs.

Although fragments are common in speech, notes, rough drafts, and writing that imitates speech, fragments should be used only for special emphasis in formal writing.

Without Subjects or Verbs

Correct a fragment that lacks a subject or verb by supplying the missing element or by combining the fragment with a complete sentence.

Lacking Subjects

A fragment without a subject may be a verb phrase (a free-standing predicate or complement); it may also be a verbal phrase (a phrase using a gerund, a participle, or an infinitive). Eliminate a fragment lacking a subject either by adding a subject or by joining the fragment to an appropriate sentence.

During the Civil War, Clara Barton organized nursing care in makeshift hospitals. ~~A~~lso founded the Red Cross. [*She* inserted before "Also"]

[A subject has been added.]

Clara Barton ~~had~~'s one overriding goal~~.~~, ~~T~~was to provide medical care to soldiers in the field.

[The infinitive phrase is joined to the sentence.]

Lacking Verbs

A fragment without a verb is usually a subject and related modifiers, an appositive, or an absolute phrase. Correct a fragment lacking a verb by adding a verb or by joining the appositive or absolute phrase to another sentence.

Dragnet, a popular police drama during the 1950s~~.~~, ~~I~~it developed a strong following during its eight years on NBC.

[The fragment has been joined to a related sentence.]

Subordinate Clauses

A subordinate clause must be joined to an independent clause to form a grammatical sentence. Correct a subordinate-clause fragment by dropping the subordinating conjunction to form a simple sentence or by joining the subordinate clause to an independent clause.

Many people with mental health problems do not seek help~~.~~ Because the stigma is sometimes too great~~.~~,

[The subordinate clause becomes part of a complex sentence.]

Special Uses of Fragments

A fragment can be effective and acceptable when it is used to isolate and thus emphasize a key word or phrase. Use this strategy selectively to achieve emphasis or to supply an answer to a question.

    Olivia Benson, Temperance Brennan, Christine Cagney, Allison Dubois, Jessica Fletcher, Brenda Johnson, Mary Beth Lacey, and Jane Tennison. These female characters populate crime dramas and help to create the strong followings that their shows garner. Do they resemble the real detectives who work in the real world?

Of course not. But viewers look to crime dramas for entertainment, not for documentary accuracy.

The opening fragment is used for emphasis; the second provides an answer to a question.

C2 Comma Splices and Fused Sentences

Comma splices and fused sentences contain two or more independent clauses that are not properly punctuated. In a comma splice (also called a comma fault), the independent clauses are incorrectly joined with only a comma. In a fused sentence (also called a run-on sentence), independent clauses are placed one after the other with no punctuation.

Correct comma splices and fused sentences by changing the punctuation or the structure of the sentence.

Forming Two Sentences

Correct a comma splice or a fused sentence by forming two sentences.

More elderly Americans than people realize suffer from early-onset Alzheimer's disease, they are often seen as merely forgetful.

Using a Semicolon

Correct a comma splice or a fused sentence by using a semicolon to separate the independent clauses.

Most industrialized countries have national health care; the United States is a notable exception.

Using Coordinating and Subordinating Conjunctions

Use a coordinating conjunction (*and, but, for, nor, or, so,* or *yet*) with a comma to link independent clauses to form a compound sentence. As an alternative, use a subordinating conjunction (*although, because, since, while,* or others) to join independent clauses to form complex or compound-complex sentences.

Comma Splice

because
The Department of Homeland Security raised the security levels/ internet "chatter" suggested that terrorist activity was possible.

[When the subordinate clause ends the sentence, a comma is unnecessary if the meaning is clear.]

Fused Sentence

Although
~~P~~olice work is sometimes intense and stressful⌄ it is more frequently procedural and mundane.

[When the subordinate clause begins the sentence, a comma is required.]

Conjunctive Adverbs

A conjunctive adverb (*besides, furthermore, however, nevertheless, still, then, therefore,* and others) connects ideas logically but does not link independent clauses grammatically. When a conjunctive adverb appears in a comma splice or fused sentence, correct the sentence by using a period or semicolon to separate the independent clauses.

Teachers and administrators usually work well together⌄ however, their unique perspectives sometimes create tension.

[The use of a semicolon grammatically separates the two independent clauses.]

C3 Pronoun Reference

To create variety and unity in your writing, substitute pronouns for overused nouns, following accepted patterns of pronoun usage.

Unclear Pronoun References

An unclear pronoun reference results when an antecedent is ambiguously placed, broad or vague, or implied rather than stated.

Ambiguous References

An ambiguous reference results when more than one noun could be a pronoun's antecedent.

Ambiguous

> Even though Patrick would only be working part time, the administrator gave him a detailed history of the prison facility. *He* thought the lecture was a waste of time.
> [Did the administrator feel dissatisfied, or did Patrick?]

Clear

> Even though he thought the lecture was a waste of time, the administrator gave Patrick a detailed history of the prison facility.
> [The rule of nearness suggests that *he* refers to the administrator.]

Vague References

A vague reference results when an antecedent is general or broad.

Vague

> During the hearing, representatives of the Centers for Disease Control and Prevention presented information about the success of education programs and requested a larger budget. *This* was approved by Congress.
> [Did Congress approve of the education programs' success, or did Congress approve the larger budget?]

Clear

> At the request of representatives of the Centers for Disease Control and Prevention, Congress approved a larger budget.

Implied References

An implied antecedent suggests a reference but does so confusingly.

Unclear

> The Booneville Educational Center is neither efficient nor organized, but *they* manage to deliver effective tutorials and workshops.
> [*They* has no direct and clear antecedent.]

Clear

> Although the director of the Booneville Educational Center is neither efficient nor organized, he manages to hire instructors who deliver effective tutorials and workshops.

Reflexive Pronouns and Subjects of Sentences

A reflexive pronoun serves only as an indirect or direct object.

> While acknowledging the important work of first responders and ambulance staff, Dr. McDonald rightfully gave *herself* credit for establishing the ER procedures that probably saved the patients' lives.

Use a personal pronoun in place of a reflexive pronoun if the subject of the sentence is not the antecedent. A reflexive pronoun should never be the subject of a sentence.

Incorrect

> Laura and *myself* disagree about the ethics of using the writing of incarcerated students in our scholarly work, whether attributed or not.

Correct

Laura and *I* disagree about the ethics of using the writing of incarcerated students in our scholarly work, whether attributed or not.

Clear Pronoun References

When a pronoun and its antecedent are separated by too many words, references become vague or unclear. Additionally, when too many pronouns are used sequentially, the writing becomes repetitive. To avoid potential confusion and to improve style, alternate between using a noun and using a pronoun. Such use also helps to establish clarity and to avoid monotony.

Jonas Salk, a researcher and virologist, is best known for the discovery of the polio vaccine. After *he* graduated from New York University School of Medicine, ~~he~~ *Salk* chose to research rather than to practice medicine. While at the University of Pittsburgh's School of Medicine, *he* began work on a polio vaccine. ~~He~~ *Salk* assembled an exceptional research team, and *he* initiated the largest clinical trial in history—involving 1,800,000 children. Although ~~he~~ *Salk* was clearly proud of *his* important contribution, *he* always acknowledged the work of others, and *he* did not seek a patent for the polio vaccine. Rather, ~~he~~ *Salk* continued *his* professional work: *he* wrote four books, and *he* worked on an HIV vaccine during *his* last years.

[Although the entire paragraph is about Salk and consequently is not confusing, it is improved by alternating Salk's name with pronouns.]

For clarity, observe the convention of restricting pronoun references to sentences *within the same paragraph*, even when the reference seems clear.

The tradition of selflessness that ~~he~~ *Salk* represented so well is challenged today by researchers—and even research institutions—who thrive on publicity and strive to garner profits. . . .

C4 Pronoun Case

The case of a pronoun indicates the pronoun's grammatical relationship to the other words in the sentence. Pronoun case is indicated by changes in form (*I*, *me*, or *mine*, for example) or by changes in position in the sentence, as in the following example.

subj. case		obj. case	poss. case	
I	gave	them	his	address.

Pronoun Case

A pronoun used as a subject or as a predicate pronoun (a pronoun used in place of a predicate noun) is in the subjective case. A pronoun used as a direct object, indirect object, or object of a preposition is in the objective case. A noun or pronoun used to show ownership is in the possessive case.

Case Forms of Personal Pronouns

	SUBJECTIVE	OBJECTIVE	POSSESSIVE
Singular			
1st person	I	me	my, mine
2nd person	you	you	your, yours
3rd person (including the singular they)	he, she, it, they	him, her, it, them	his, her, hers, its, their, theirs
Plural			
1st person	we	us	our, ours
2nd person	you	you	your, yours
3rd person	they	them	their, theirs

Case Forms of *Who* and Related Pronouns

SUBJECTIVE	OBJECTIVE	POSSESSIVE
who	whom	whose
whoever	whomever	

Usually a pronoun changes form to produce the possessive case (*I*, *my*; *she*, *her*); however, an indefinite pronoun (*someone*, *everybody*) forms the possessive by adding *'s* (*someone's*, *everybody's*).

A possessive-case pronoun, which does not use an apostrophe, should not be confused with a contraction that sounds the same: *its* and *it's* ("it is"), *theirs* and *there's* ("there is"), and *whose* and *who's* ("who is").

Subjective Case

A pronoun used as the subject of a sentence or clause is in the subjective case.

Subjective Case

Although *she* began her career as a lawyer, Janet Napolitano's work as a judge, attorney general, and governor prepared her well for her role as Secretary of the Department of Homeland Security.

When a sentence has a compound subject, isolate the parts of the subject to help you choose the appropriate pronoun.

Compound Subject

Warren Burger and William Rehnquist were the longest-serving Chief Justices of the Supreme Court. Burger and *he* served six years longer than other justices in the 20th century.
 [Burger served; *he* served; consequently, *Burger and he served*.]

Because a predicate pronoun restates the subject, it requires the subjective case. If this construction sounds too formal, invert the subject and the predicate pronoun.

During triage, we learned that the chief organizer was *he*.
 [The predicate pronoun, signaled by the linking verb *was*, must be in the subjective case.]

During triage, we learned that *he* was the chief organizer.
 [This sentence sounds less formal.]

Objective Case

A pronoun used as a direct object or as an indirect object must be in the objective case.

Direct Object

In developing the fourth amendment to the U.S. Constitution, the founders established protections against unreasonable searches and seizures; we should honor *them* for that.

Indirect Object

Although judges who deny search warrants may seem to protect suspected criminals, we should give *them* credit for protecting individual rights.

Object of Preposition

People from all walks of life surely realize that the fourth amendment establishes essential protections for *them*.

When a preposition has a compound object, isolate the parts of the object to help you select the appropriate pronoun.

After the terrorist attacks on September 11, 2001, President Bush and Attorney General Ashcroft pushed for legislation that to some degree compromises the fourth amendment. Although many law makers were involved, most of the attention was directed at *him* and Ashcroft.
[at *him*; at Ashcroft]

Possessive Case

Possessive Pronouns Used With Nouns

A possessive pronoun—*my*, *your*, *his*, *her*, *its*, *our*, *your*, or *their*—modifies a noun. It acts as an adjective and is sometimes called a pronoun-adjective.

> Tamika and Marcus received the same grades in classes and the same evaluations for clinicals. However, *her* scores on the Board exam were slightly better than *his* results.
> [The pronouns in the possessive case serve as pronoun-adjectives.]

Possessive Pronouns Used Alone

The possessive pronouns *mine*, *yours*, *his*, *hers*, *its*, *ours*, *yours*, or *theirs* are sometimes used alone. Each can act as a subject, predicate pronoun, direct object, or object of a preposition.

> Given the size of the crowd and the physical irregularity of the location, the responsibility for the lack of perimeter control was only partly *theirs*.

Possessive Pronouns Modifying a Gerund

When modifying a gerund (an *-ing* verb that functions as a noun), a pronoun must be in the possessive case, serving as a pronoun-adjective.

> I was annoyed by *his* snickering during the parent–teacher conference.
> [The annoyance resulted from the person's *snickering*, not from the person himself.]

> The supervisor commented that *their* handling of paperwork was both timely and meticulous.
> [The best part was their *handling of paperwork*, not them.]

Appositives and Elliptical Constructions

Pronouns in Appositives

When a pronoun is part of an appositive that restates the subject of a clause, the pronoun is in the subjective case. When it restates an object, the pronoun is in the objective case.

> The two precinct captains, *she* and Gerald, were responsible for preparing the weekly reports.
> [Because the phrase *she and Gerald* restates the subject of the sentence (*two precinct captains*), the pronoun must be in the subjective case.]

> The chief of police sent a memo stating that recommendations for procedural changes be sent to the precinct captains, Gerald and *her*.
> [*Gerald and her* restates *precinct captains*, the object of the preposition *to*; therefore, the pronoun must be in the objective case.]

We or Us With Nouns

When using *we* or *us* with a noun, choose the case that would be correct if the noun were omitted.

> The cliché is true: *We* Americans take many of our freedoms for granted.
> [Without *Americans*, the pronoun appears correctly in the subjective case.]

Pronouns in Elliptical Constructions

An elliptical construction (a construction in which words are omitted or understood) uses the case that would be appropriate if all the words were included. If the pronoun used alone sounds too formal, add the omitted words.

> The clinic's stress counselor arrived twenty minutes later than *we*.
> [It is understood that the counselor arrived twenty minutes later than *we arrived*.]

Who and Whoever and Whom and Whomever

Who and Whoever

Use the subjective-case form—*who* or *whoever*—as the subject of a sentence, clause, or question.

Jack Kevorkian, a pathologist *who* supported physician-assisted suicide, was commonly known in the media as "Dr. Death."

[*Who* is the subject of the clause.]

Like most confrontational activists, Kevorkian would make frank and often startling observations to *whoever* would listen—reporters, interviewers, or commentators.

[*Whoever* is the subject of the clause; although the preposition *to* might suggest that the objective case is required, the whole clause, not the word *whoever*, is the object of the preposition.]

Whom and *Whomever*

Use the objective-case form—*whom* or *whomever*—as a direct object, indirect object, or object of a preposition.

Whom should we propose for the vacant seat on the advisory board of the Community Safety Council?

[*Whom* is the direct object of *propose*.]

The board will probably appoint *whomever* we select.

[*Whomever* is the direct object of *select*.]

C5 Positioning Modifiers

Position modifiers—which explain, describe, define, or limit a word or group of words—so that the relationship between them and the words they modify is clear.

Clarity and Smoothness

Place modifiers where they create clear meaning.

Long Modifiers

If a long modifier separates the subject from the verb or the verb from the object, reposition the modifier.

Jeffrey Toobin's *The Nine: Inside the Secret World of the Supreme Court*, a behind-closed-doors account of the workings of the nation's highest court, is both fascinating and informative.

Prepositional Phrases

Because nearness guides modification, place prepositional phrases near the words they modify.

Because of her controversial positions on drug use and contraception, Dr. Mildred Jefferson criticized Dr. Joycelyn Elders's work as Surgeon General.

[Elders, not Jefferson, held the controversial views.]

Limiting Modifiers

Place limiting modifiers such as *hardly*, *nearly*, or *only* with care and double-check to see that the meaning of the sentence is clear.

> He simply stated the problem.
>   [Stating the problem is all he did.]
>
> He stated the problem simply.
>   [He made the problem easy to understand.]

Modifiers Near Infinitives

Under most circumstances, do not position a modifier between the elements of an infinitive: *to* and a verb. Although this usage is common in speech and some kinds of writing, it is best to avoid split infinitives.

After rereading his notes, Dr. Martinez began to quickly prepare his report.

Dangling Modifiers

When a phrase at the beginning of a sentence does not modify the subject of the sentence, it is a dangling modifier. Reposition the misplaced phrase.

Alternately celebratory or outraged, the courtroom erupted with reactions from the people present.

[The people, not the courtroom, had strong reactions.]

Squinting Modifiers

A squinting modifier is a word or phrase that could modify either the words before it or the words after it. Reposition the element to avoid confusion or use the relative pronoun *that* to clarify your meaning.

The mediator said ~~before ten o'clock~~ they could conclude the proceedings∧.

[This repositioning clarifies a ten o'clock conclusion of the proceedings; alternately, moving the phrase *before ten o'clock* to the beginning of the sentence would emphasize the time at which the mediator spoke.]

C6   Active and Passive Voice

Active and passive voice establishes the significance of main ideas and helps to create focus in writing. Consequently, the choices you make control your meaning.

Active and Passive Sentences

Active Sentences

In an active sentence, the subject of the sentence acts.

Transportation Security Administration officers now screen passengers using full-body scanners.

Passive Sentences

In a passive sentence, the subject of the sentence is acted upon. A passive verb requires auxiliaries. While a passive sentence does not always specify the person completing the action, when it does, the person is named in a prepositional phrase beginning with *by*.

Passengers are now screened by Transportation Security Administration officers using full-body scanners.

Emphasis: Who or What Acts

An active sentence emphasizes the doer of an action. It establishes a clear, strong relationship between the subject and verb.

The patient's lifestyle clearly compromised her general health.
[The patient's compromised health is clearly due to her choices.]

When the results of an action are more important than the doer of the action or when the doer is unknown, passive sentences effectively express the meaning.

The patient's health was further compromised by a misdirected care plan.

Using an active or a passive verb allows subtle but significant shifts in meaning and emphasis.

Active

In 2007, criminals stole an estimated $16 billion in property in the United States.
[The use of *criminals* with the active verb *stole* emphasizes the actions of criminals.]

Passive

An estimated $16 billion in property was stolen in the United States in 2007.
[This sentence shifts the emphasis to the value of the stolen property.]

Emphasis: Repeated Action

The passive voice emphasizes the action over the doer of the action; thus, it is especially useful for describing universal or widespread conditions or events.

Passive

Having a colonoscopy is now a common procedure for people over 50.
[The procedure is most important here, not the individual doctors who perform it.]

Active

Doctors commonly perform colonoscopies on people over 50.
[This construction emphasizes the doctors who perform the procedures.]

Generally, write active sentences when "who is doing what" is most important. When "what is being done" is most important, passive sentences serve your purpose better.

C7 Possessives and Contractions

Use apostrophes to show possession (usually with an added s) and to indicate the omission of letters or numbers from words or dates.

Possessives and Contractions

Possessive Case

Singular Nouns

Form the possessive of a singular noun (either common or proper) by adding 's, even when the singular noun ends in s (bus's seats, Frances's nickname).

COMMON NOUNS	PROPER NOUNS
operating room's features	Atticus's closing arguments
boss's recommendations	B. F. Skinner's legacy
building's perimeter	New Orleans's hospitals

Plural Nouns

Form the possessive of a plural noun (either common or proper) ending in s by adding an apostrophe only; an additional s is unnecessary. Form the possessive of an irregular plural noun that does not end in s (*children*, for example) by adding 's.

teachers' lounge   the Madoffs' legal counsel
But:
children's advocates   women's rights

To check whether a possessive form is correct, eliminate the s or just the apostrophe. The word remaining should be the correct one for your meaning. For example, the phrase *student's complaints* refers to only one student; the phrase *students' complaints* refers to multiple students.

Compound Words and Joint Possession

Form the possessive of a compound word or indicate joint possession in a series by adding 's to the last noun only.

brother-in-law's surgery
New York, Los Angeles, and Chicago's combined crime statistics

If possession in a series is not joint but individual, each noun in the series must be possessive.

Meirhold's, Vandes's, and Chaney's fingerprints
[Each person has a separate set of fingerprints.]

Omission of Letters and Numbers

Use an apostrophe to form a contraction and to create an abbreviated version of a date, with some of the numbers omitted.

Contractions and abbreviated dates are best used in informal writing. In formal writing, present names and dates fully.

WITH APOSTROPHE	COMPLETE FORM
shouldn't	should not
I'll	I will or I shall
the '98 report	the 1998 report

Not With Possessive Pronouns

Do not use an apostrophe with a possessive pronoun. Do not be confused by those that end in –s (*yours*, *ours*, *his*, and others).

The child's parents completed the family-history questionnaire; the information was *theirs*.

[not *their's*].

The medical technician asked for clarifications and entered the information into the database; the responsibility for the completed work was *hers*.

[not *her's*].

[Apostrophes in *their's* and *her's* would indicate contracted forms—*their is* and *her is*—which are nonsensical. Clearly, the possessive pronouns are correct.]

C8 Outlining

An outline is a structural plan using headings and subdivisions to clarify the main features of the paper and the interrelationships among them. Loosely structured, informal outlines provide simplicity and freedom, while highly systematic, formal outlines emphasize clarity and completeness.

In the earliest stages of drafting—when you are deciding what should come first, second, third, and so on—an informal outline works well. At later stages of writing—when you need to analyze your work for consistency, completeness, and logic—a formal outline is helpful. Importantly, informal and formal outlines are plans, not descriptions of what you *must* do. If your plan does not work, decide why and make the necessary changes.

An Informal Outline

An informal outline is intended for your use only. Consequently, it may follow a pattern that is uniquely yours, as long as it is consistent. Consider creating lists marked with numbers, arrows dots, dashes, or any other convenient symbol to indicate relative importance among ideas.

This is a brief, informal outline for a paper on two important pieces of medical equipment.

Stethoscope (1816)
- René Laënnec
- Description
- Improvements
  - Golding Bird
  - Arthur Leared
  - George Cammann

Blood Pressure Meter (1881)
- Samuel Siegfried Karl Ritter von Basch
- Description
- Improvements
  - Scipione Riva-Rocci
  - Harvey Cushing

This is an informal outline for a paper on four particular murder trials.

Harry Thaw (1906)
- Thaw
- White
- Newspaper coverage

Leopold and Loeb (1924)
- Leopold and Loeb
- Bobby Franks
- Newspaper and radio coverage

Bruno Hauptmann (1935)
- Hauptmann
- The Lindbergh baby
- Newspaper and radio coverage

O. J. Simpson (1995)
- Simpson
- Nicole Brown and Ron Goldman
- Newspaper, radio, television, and internet coverage

A Formal Outline

A formal outline is intended for readers. For this reason, it must adhere to the following conventions.

- Indicate major topics with uppercase Roman numerals (I, II, III).
- Indicate subdivisions of topics with uppercase letters (A, B, C).
- Indicate clarifications of subdivisions (examples, supporting facts, and so on) with Arabic numerals (1, 2, 3).
- Indicate details with lowercase letters (a, b, c).

In addition, a formal outline must adhere to the following structural conventions.

- **Use parallel forms throughout.** Use phrases and words in a topic outline and full sentences in a sentence outline. An outline may use full sentences for major topics and phrases in subdivisions of topics (a mixed outline) but should do so consistently.
- **Include only one idea in each entry.** Subdivide entries that contain more than one idea.
- **Include at least two entries at each sublevel.** If the topic can't be subdivided, then simply use the main element.
- **Indicate the inclusion of introductions and conclusions but do not outline their content.** Although they are important to the overall effect of the paper, introductions and conclusions are identified but not described. If you wish to include a thesis statement or research question, identify it clearly after the label for the introduction and before the formal outline begins.
- **Align headings of the same level at the same margin.** When reviewing a formal outline, readers expect to find similar material presented in a similar way. Use consistent indentation patterns in the formal outline to show this degree of emphasis.

The formal outline presented next is a developed version of the informal outline on medical equipment that is included on page 175.

INTRODUCTION

Thesis Statement: The invention of two pieces of medical equipment revolutionized the ways in which patients are examined.

  I. Stethoscope (1816)
     A. René Laënnec
        1. French physician
        2. Necker-Enfants Malades Hospital
     B. Description
        1. Wooden tube
        2. Flanges at both ends
        3. Monoaural (one ear)
        4. Resembled an "ear trumpet"

C. Improvements
　　　　1. Golding Bird (1840)
　　　　　　a. Flexible tubing
　　　　　　b. Still monoaural
　　　　2. Arthur Leared (1851)
　　　　　　a. Biaural (two ear)
　　　　　　b. Improved earpieces
　　　　3. George Cammann (1852)
　　　　　　a. Refined design
　　　　　　b. For commercial production
II. Blood Pressure Meter (1881)
　　A. Samuel Siegfried Karl Ritter von Basch
　　　　1. Austrian physician
　　　　2. University of Vienna
　　B. Description
　　　　1. A cuff
　　　　2. Measuring unit/gauge
　　　　3. Inflation bulb and valve
　　C. Improvements
　　　　1. Scipione Riva-Rocci (1896)
　　　　　　a. Improved design
　　　　　　b. Easier use
　　　　2. Harvey Cushing (1901)
　　　　　　a. Refined design
　　　　　　b. Promoted it commercially

CONCLUSION

The following formal outline is a developed version of the informal outline on murder trials that is included on page 175.

INTRODUCTION

Thesis Statement: America's fascination with wealth and privilege has often led to an inordinate interest in murder trials that involved people with money.

　　I. Harry Kendal Thaw (1906)
　　　　A. Thaw (defendant)
　　　　　　1. Son of a wealthy industrialist
　　　　　　2. History of mental problems
　　　　　　3. Married to an actress who knew White

- B. Stanford White (victim)
    1. Partner in McKim, Mead, and White—a prestigious architectural firm
    2. Known for his lavish lifestyle
    3. Known for womanizing
- C. Sensational newspaper stories

II. Nathan Leopold, Jr., and Richard Loeb (1924)
- A. Leopold and Loeb (murderers)
    1. Sons of wealthy businessmen
    2. Students at University of Michigan and University of Chicago
    3. Lovers
- B. Bobby Franks (victim)
    1. Son of Chicago millionaire
    2. Kidnapped
    3. Possibly tortured
    4. Killed
- C. Sensational newspaper and radio stories

III. Bruno Hauptmann (1935)
- A. Hauptmann (alleged murderer)
    1. German immigrant
    2. Some circumstantial evidence
- B. Child of Charles Lindbergh (victim)
    1. Son of the famous aviator
    2. Kidnapped from his bedroom
    3. Murdered
- C. Sensational newspaper and radio stories

IV. O. J. Simpson (1995)
- A. Simpson (alleged murderer)
    1. Famous football player
    2. Celebrity status
- B. Nicole Brown and Ronald Goldman (victims)
    1. Simpson's ex-wife
    2. Brown's friend
    3. Killed outside her condominium
- C. Sensational newspaper, radio, television, and internet coverage

CONCLUSION

Index

Abbreviations, acceptable, 69
Abstract, 28, 29–30
  citing, 80
  online, 108–109
Active and passive voice, 56, 171–172
  active sentences, 56, 171–172
  emphasis, 171–172
    repeated action for, 172
    who or what acts, 171–172
  passive sentences, 56, 171–172
Afterword, citing, 93
Agreement, 56–57
  pronoun-antecedent agreement, 57
  subject-verb agreement, 56–57
Alphabetizing reference list, 69–70
Ambiguous reference, 162
Annotated bibliography, 139–145
  content of, annotations, 140–141
  creating, elements, 141–142
  format guidelines
    annotations, positioning, 140
    general guidelines, 139–140
  planning annotations, 141
  sample annotation, 143–145
APA editorial style, 41–62
  general style, 54–58
    agreement, 56–57
    parallelism, 58
    transitions, 55
    verb tense, 55–56
  punctuation and mechanics, 41–54
    brackets, 47–48
    capitalization, 48–51
    colons, 43
    commas, 42
    dashes, 44
    hyphens, 44–46
    italics, 51–52
    number style, 52–54
    parentheses, 46
    periods, 41–42
    quotation marks, 46
    semicolons, 42–43
    slashes, 48
  word choice, 58–62
    biased language, 60–62
    colloquialisms, 59
    jargon, 59
    noun clusters, 58
    specificity, 59–60
APA manuscript, 27–40
  guidelines, 36–40
    font selection, 36–37
    headings for sections, 38–40
    line spacing, 37
    margins and indentations, 37–38

Index

APA manuscript (*continued*)
  paging (running head), 38
  paper, 36
  seriation, 38, 54
  submitting the paper, 40
  word spacing, 37
 parts of, 27–32
  abstract, 29–30
  appendices, 36
  figures, 34–35
  footnotes, 32–33
  reference list, 31–32
  tables, 33–34
  text, 30–31
  title page, 27–28
Apostrophe with possessive pronoun, 174
Appendices, 36
Appositives, 168
  pronouns in, 168
  we or *us* with noun, 168
Art, work of, citing, 101
Articles, citing
 online articles
  in online encyclopedia or reference work, 109
  in online journal, 106
  in online magazine, 106
  in online newsletter, 107
  in online newspaper, 106–107
 print articles
  in encyclopedia or other reference work, 91
  in journal, 80
  in monthly magazine, 81
  in newsletter, 82
  in newspaper, 81–82
  in weekly magazine, 81
Audio podcast, citing, 112
Audiovisual sources, citing, 97–102
  film, 97–98
  interview, 100
  lecture or speech, 101
  map, graph, table, or chart, 101–102
  radio broadcast, 99
  recording, 99–100
  slide set or filmstrip, 98
  television broadcast, 98–99
  work of art, 101
Audiovisual sources, evaluating, 13
Authors, citing books by
  book by one author, 86
  book by two or more authors, 86–87
  book with no author named, 87
  book with organization as author, 87–88
  multiple works by same author, 95–96

Biased language, 60–62
  gender bias, 61–62
  in historical context, 62
  other forms of bias, 62
  preferred racial or ethnic terms, 60–61
  racial and ethnic bias, 60
Bibliography, annotated, 139–145

Index

Blog posting, citing, 113
Book by one author, citing, 86
Book by two or more authors, citing, 86–87
Book with no author named, citing, 87
Book with organization as author, citing, 87–88
Books and other separately published materials, citing, 85–96
   afterword, 93
   article in encyclopedia or other reference work, 91
   book by one author, citing, 86
   book by two or more authors, citing, 86–87
   book with no author named, citing, 87
   book with organization as author, citing, 87–88
   edited collection, 88
   edition other than first, 88
   epilogue, 93
   forward, 93
   government document (committee, commission, department), 92
   introduction, 93
   monograph, 93
   multiple works by same author, 95–96
   multivolume work, 90–91
   original selection in edited collection, 88–89
   pamphlet, brochure, or fact sheet, 94
   preface, 93
   previously published selection in edited collection, 89–90
   published proceedings from conference, 94–95
   reprinted book, 90
   revised or enlarged edition, 90
   secondary source, 96
   translation, 92
   unpublished dissertations, 94
Brackets, 47–48
Brochure, citing, 94

Capitalization, 48–51
   headline case, 48
   headline-style capitalization, 51
   no capitalization, examples, 49
   sentence case, 48
   sentence-style capitalization, 51
   title case, 48
   of titles, 50
   uses of, examples, 48–49
Cardinal numbers, 54
Careless plagiarism, 17
Case forms
   of personal pronouns, 165
   of *who* and related pronouns, 165

Index

CD-ROM source, citing, 111
Chart, citing, 101–102
   online, 110–111
Citations. *see* Parenthetical citations
Colloquialisms, 59
Colons, 43
Comma splices and fused sentences, 161–162
   conjunctive adverbs, 162
   forming two sentences, 161
   using coordinating or subordinating conjunctions, 161–162
   using semicolon, 161
Commas, 42
   in numbers, 54
Common knowledge, 18–19
Conclusion in outline, 176–178
Conjunctive adverbs, 162
Contractions. *see* Possessives and contractions
Coordinating conjunctions, 161–162
Copy-and-paste plagiarism, 17
Course-related goals, 4

Dangling modifiers, 170
Dashes, 44
Direct object, 166
Discussion group posting, citing, 113
Dissertation, citing, 94
   online, 108
DOI (digital object identifier), 7, 104

Drafting, writing strategies for
   general paper, 23
   research paper, 23–24

Edited collection, citing, 88
   original selection in, 88–89
   previously published selection in, 89–90
Edition other than first, citing, 88
Editorial, citing, 82–83
Electronic sources, citing, 103–113
   articles
      in online encyclopedia or reference work, 109
      in online journal, 106
      in online magazine, 106
      in online newsletter, 107
      in online newspaper, 106–107
   audio podcast, 112
   CD-ROM source, 111
   email interview, 111
   online abstract, 108–109
   online book, 107–108
   online dissertation or thesis, 108
   online map, graph, table, or chart, 110–111
   online transcript of lecture or speech, 110
   online video, 112
   posting to blog, discussion group, Facebook, or Twitter, 113

Index

principles for citing, 104–105
specialized online sources, 105
website or scholarly project, 109–110
Ellipsis points, 78
Elliptical constructions, 168
Email interview, citing, 111
Emphasis, 171–172
repeated action for, 172
who or what acts, 171–172
Encyclopedia, citing articles in, 91
online, 109
Enlarged edition, citing, 90
Epilogue, citing, 93
Ethnic bias, 60
Ethnic terms, preferred, 60–61
Evaluating sources, 10–14
audiovisual sources, 13
combinations of sources, 14
internet sources, 12–13
print sources, 10–11

Facebook posting, citing, 113
Fact note, 16
Fact sheet, citing, 94
Figures, 34–35
Film, citing, 97–98
Filmstrip, citing, 98
Font selection, 36–37
Footnotes, 32
placing note numbers in the paper, 32–33
Formal outline, 175–178
Format for APA entries, 66–69
Forward, citing, 93

Fragments, 159–161
special uses of, 160–161
subordinate clauses, 160
without subjects, 159–160
without verbs, 160
Fused sentences. *see* Comma splices and fused sentences

Gender bias, 61–62
Gerund, 167
Goals (research), 4–5
Government document (committee, commission, department), citing, 92
Graph, citing, 101–102
online, 110–111
Graphic design in PowerPoint presentation, 150–153

Headings for sections, 38–40
Headline case, 48
Headline-style capitalization, 51
HTML (hypertext markup language), 8
Hypertext markup language (HTML), 8
Hyphens, 44–46
Hypothesis, 3
planning, 22

Implied reference, 163
Indentations, 37–38
Indirect object, 166
Infinitives, modifiers near, 170

Informal outline, 174–175
Information databases, as information source, 105
Information for APA entries, 64–66
Internet research, 9–10
Internet sources, evaluating, 12–13
Interview, citing, 100
In-text citations. *see* Parenthetical citations
Introduction
   citing, 93
   in outline, 176, 177
Italics, 51–52

Jargon, 59
Journals, citing, 80

Lecture, citing, 101
   online transcript of, 110
Letter to editor, citing, 83
Letters, omission of, 173–174
Library, 5–6
Limiting modifiers, 170
Line spacing, 37
Long modifiers, 169

Magazine, monthly, citing, 81
   online, 106
Magazine, weekly, citing, 81
Map, citing, 101–102
   online, 110–111
Margins and indentations, 37–38
Mechanics. *see* Punctuation and mechanics
Modifiers, positioning, 169–171

clarity and smoothness, 169–170
dangling modifiers, 170
limiting modifiers, 170
long modifiers, 169
modifiers near infinitives, 170
prepositional phrases, 170
squinting modifiers, 170–171
Monograph, citing, 93
Monthly magazine, citing, 81
   online, 106
Motion picture. *see* Film, citing
Multiple works by same author, citing, 95–96
Multivolume work, citing, 90–91

Newsletter, citing, 82
   online, 107
Newspaper, citing, 81–82
   online, 106–107
No capitalization, examples of, 49
Note-taking, 14–17
   complete information, 15
   consistent format, 15–16
   kinds of notes, 16
   methods of, 15
   reviewing, 21
   sample note card, 16–17, 20–21
Noun clusters, 58
Nouns
   plural, 173

possessive pronouns with, 167
singular, 173
we or *us* with, 168
Number style, 52–54
cardinal numbers, 54
commas in numbers, 54
numbered seriation, 38, 54
ordinal numbers, 54
plurals of numbers, 54
uses of numerals, examples, 52–53
uses of words for numbers, examples, 53
Numbered seriation, 38, 54
Numbers, omission of, 173–174

Objective case, 166–167
direct object, 166
indirect object, 166
object of preposition, 166–167
Object of preposition, 166–167
Objective, stated, 3
planning, 22
Online abstract, citing, 108–109
Online articles
in online encyclopedia or reference work, 109
in online journal, 106
in online magazine, 106
in online newsletter, 107
in online newspaper, 106–107
Online book, citing, 107–108

Online catalogs, 8–9
format options, 8
Online chart, citing, 110–111
Online dissertation or thesis, citing, 108
Online graph, citing, 110–111
Online map, citing, 110–111
Online posting to blog, discussion group, Facebook, or Twitter, 113
Online sources, specialized, 105
information databases, 105
scholarly projects, 105
Online table, citing, 110–111
Online transcripts, citing, 110
Online video, citing, 112
Ordinal numbers, 54
Organization, as author, 87–88
Organization, planning, 22
Original selection in edited collection, citing, 88–89
Outlining, 174–178
formal outline, 175–178
informal outline, 174–175

Paging (running head), 38
Pamphlet, citing, 94
Paper, 36
Parallelism, 58
Paraphrase note, 16
Parentheses, 46
Parenthetical capitalization, 50
Parenthetical citations, 71–74
basic forms of, 71–74
patterns for, 71, 73–74

Index

Passive voice. *see* Active and passive voice
PDF (portable document format), 8
Periodical databases and online catalogs, 6–9
  format options, 8
  information about books and other library-based materials, 8–9
  information about periodicals, 6–8
Periodicals, citing, 79–84
  abstract, 80
  articles
    in journal, 80
    in monthly magazine, 81
    in newsletter, 82
    in newspaper, 81–82
    in weekly magazine, 81
  editorial, 82–83
  letter to editor, 83
  review, 83
  secondary source, 84
Periods, 41–42
Personal goals, 5
Personal pronouns, case forms of, 165
Plagiarism, 17–21
  acceptable paraphrase, sample of, 22
  acceptable summary, sample of, 21
  careless plagiarism, 17
  common knowledge, 18–19
  copy-and-paste plagiarism, 17
  faulty paraphrase, sample of, 21
  faulty summary, sample of, 20
  special qualities of source materials, 19–20
  whole-paper plagiarism, 17
Planning, 21–22
  hypothesis, 22
  organization, 22
  reviewing notes, 21
  stated objective, 22
  thesis statement, 22
Plurals of numbers, 54
Portable document format (PDF), 8
Possessive case, 167, 172–174
  compound words and joint possession, 173
  plural nouns, 173
  possessive pronouns modifying a gerund, 167
  possessive pronouns used alone, 167
  possessive pronouns used with nouns, 167
  possessive pronouns with apostrophe, 174
  singular nouns, 173
Possessives and contractions, 172–174
  apostrophe with possessive pronoun, 174
  omission of letters and numbers, 173–174
  possessive case, 173
Poster presentations, 155–158

features of, identifying, 156–157
planning for, 157
sample poster, 158
thinking about preparing and delivering, 155–156
Postings, citing
blog, 113
discussion group, 113
Facebook, 113
Twitter, 113
PowerPoint presentation, 147–155
content
general considerations, 148
specific considerations, 148–150
graphic design, 150–153
performance elements of, 153–155
planning for, 147–148
technical matters, 153
thinking about preparing and delivering, 147
Preface, citing, 93
Prepositional phrases, 170
Previously published selection in edited collection, citing, 89–90
Print sources (and electronic counterparts), evaluating, 10–11
Professional goals, 4–5
Pronoun-antecedent agreement, 57
Pronoun case, 164–169
appositives, 168
case forms of personal pronouns, 165
case forms of *who* and related pronouns, 165
elliptical constructions, 168
objective case, 166–167
possessive case, 167
subjective case, 165–166
Pronoun reference, 162–164
clear, 162–164
reflexive pronouns and subjects of sentences, 163–164
unclear, 162–164
Published proceedings from conference, citing, 94–95
Publishers' names, shortening, 68
Punctuation and mechanics, 41–54
brackets, 47–48, 77–78
capitalization, 48–51
colons, 43
commas, 42
dashes, 44
hyphens, 44–46
italics, 51–52
number style, 52–54
parentheses, 46
periods, 41–42
quotation marks, 46, 76–78
in quotations, 76–78
brackets, 77–78
ellipsis points, 78
single quotation marks, 76–77

Punctuation and mechanics (*continued*)
  semicolons, 42–43
  slashes, 48

Quotation marks, 46
  in quotations, 75–77
Quotation note, 16
Quotations, 74–78
  brief, 75
  concerns about, 76
  long, 75–76
  punctuation with, 76–78
    brackets, 77–78
    ellipsis points, 78
    single quotation marks, 76–77

Racial bias, 60
Racial terms, preferred, 60–61
Radio broadcast, citing, 99
Recording, citing, 99–100
Reference list, 31–32, 63–74
  abbreviations, acceptable, 69
  alphabetizing, 69–70
  entries for audiovisual sources, 97
  entries for books and other separately published materials, 86
  entries for electronic sources, 104
  entries for periodicals, 79
  format for APA entries, 66–69
  information for APA entries, 64–66
  overview, 63
  parenthetical citations, 71–74
    basic forms of, 71–74
    patterns for, 71, 73–74
Reference-list (and other) capitalization, 50
Reference-list entries, citing
  audiovisual sources, 97–102
  books and other separately published materials, 85–96
  electronic sources, 103–113
  periodicals, 79–84
Reflexive pronouns, 163–164
Reprinted book, citing, 90
Research goals, 3–5
  course-related goals, 4
  personal goals, 5
  professional goals, 4–5
Research methods, 5–10
  internet, 9–10
  library, 5–6
  periodical databases and online catalogs, 6–9
Retrieval information, citing, 65
Review, citing, 83
Revised edition, citing, 90
Revising
  content, questions for, 24
  style, questions for, 25
  technical matters, questions for, 25
Running head, paging, 38

Sample papers, examining, 115–138
Scholarly projects, as online source, 105
Secondary source, citing, 84, 96
Semicolons, 42–43

Index

in comma splices and
fused sentences, 161
Sentence case, 48
Sentences
active, 171–172
fused, 161–162
passive, 171–172
Sentence-style capitalization, 51
Separately published materials, citing. *see* Books and other separately published materials, citing
Seriation, 38, 54
numbered, 38, 54
Slashes, 48
Slide set, citing, 98
Sources, evaluating, 10–14
audiovisual sources, 13
combinations of sources, 14
internet sources, 12–13
print sources (and electronic counterparts), 10–11
Specialized online sources, 105
Specificity, 59–60
Speech, citing, 101
online transcript of, 110
Squinting modifiers, 170–171
Stated objective, 3
planning, 22
Subjective case, 165–166
Subjects for papers, 1–2
guidelines for assessing, 1–2

narrow topic, 2
Subjects of sentences
compound, 166
fragments without, 159–160
Subject-verb agreement, 56–57
Submitting the paper, 40
Subordinate clauses, 160
Subordinating conjunctions, 161–162
Summary note, 16

Tables, 33–34
citing, 101–102
online, 110–111
Technical issues in writing, 159–178
active and passive voice, 171–172
active sentences, 171–172
passive sentences, 171–172
repeated action for emphasis, 172
comma splices and fused sentences, 161–162
conjunctive adverbs, 162
forming two sentences, 161
using coordinating or subordinating conjunctions, 161–162
using semicolon, 161
fragments, 159–161
special uses of, 160–161

Technical issues in writing (*continued*)
  subordinate clauses, 160
  without subjects or verbs, 159–160
 outlining, 174–178
  formal outline, 175–178
  informal outline, 174–175
 positioning modifiers, 169–171
  clarity and smoothness, 169–171
  dangling modifiers, 170
  squinting modifiers, 170–171
 possessives and contractions, 174
  apostrophe with possessive pronoun, 173–174
  omission of letters and numbers, 173–174
  possessive case, 173–174
 pronoun case, 164–169
  appositives, 168
  case forms of personal pronouns, 165
  case forms of *who* and related pronouns, 165
  elliptical constructions, 168
  objective case, 166–167
  possessive case, 167
  subjective case, 165–166
  who and *whoever* and *whom* and *whomever*, 168–169
 pronoun reference, 162–164
  clear pronoun references, 162–164
  reflexive pronouns and subjects of sentences, 163–164
  unclear, 162–164
Television broadcast, citing, 98–99
Text, 30–31
Thesis, online, citing, 108
Thesis statement, 3
 planning, 22
Title case, 48
Title page, 27–28
Titles, capitalization of, 50
 article title in reference-list entry, 50
 article title in text, 50
 book title in reference-list entry, 50
 book title in text, 50
Topic, narrowing, 2
Transitional words and phrases, 55
Transitions, 55
Translation, citing, 92
Twitter posting, citing, 113

Unpublished dissertation, citing, 94

Vague reference, 163
Verb tense, 55–56
Verbs, 160–161
Video online, citing, 112
Voice, active and passive. *see* Active and passive voice

We or *us* with noun, 168
Websites, as information source, 105
Weekly magazine, citing, 81
Who, case forms of, 165
Who and *whoever*, 168–169
Whole-paper plagiarism, 17
Whom and *whomever*, 168–169
Word choice, 58–62
  biased language, 60–62
  colloquialisms, 59
  jargon, 59
  noun clusters, 58
  specificity, 59–60
Word spacing, 37

Words for numbers, examples, 53
Work of art, citing, 101
Writing strategies, 22–25
  for drafting a paper, 23
  for drafting a research paper, 23–24
  questions for revising content, 24
  questions for revising style, 25
  questions for revising technical matters, 25
Writing, technical issues in. *see* Technical issues in writing

Format for APA Reference-List Entries

1. Begin the first line at the left margin and indent subsequent lines ½ inch.
2. Invert the author's name so that the last name appears first; use first and middle initials.
3. When no author is named, list the source by title.
4. Place the publication date in parentheses, followed by a period.
5. Cite the complete title, including subtitles.
6. Use a period, followed by one space, to separate author, date, title, and publication information.

See Chapters 4 to 8 for additional information and examples.

Sample Reference-List Entries

An Article in a Journal (5a)
Harrison, R. L., & Westwood, M. J. (2009). Preventing vicarious traumatization of mental health therapists: Identifying protective practices. *Psychotherapy: Theory, Research, Practice, Training, 46*(2), 203–219. https://doi.org/10.1037/a0016081

An Article in a Monthly Magazine (5c)
Gorman, C. (2010, October). Closing the health gap. *Scientific American, 303*(4), 34, 36.

An Article in a Newspaper (5e)
Pogrebin, R. (2010, April 22). A mother's loss, a daughter's story. *The New York Times*, E1, E9.

A Book by One Author (6a)
Weiner, M. F. (2010). *Power, protest, and the public school: Jewish and African American struggles in New York City.* Rutgers University Press.

A Book by Two or More Authors (6b)
Wright, J. P., Tibbetts, S. G., & Daigle, L. E. (2008). *Criminals in the making: Criminality across the life course.* Sage.

An Edition Other Than the First (6e)
Moritsugu, J., Wong, F. Y., & Duffy, K. G. (2010). *Community psychology* (4th ed.). Allyn.